OFFICE FOR STANDARDS
IN EDUCATION

Handbook for Inspecting
SECONDARY SCHOOLS

with guidance on self-evaluation

This *Handbook* applies to the inspection of schools in England from January 2000

London: The Stationery Office

ISBN 0 11 350110 2

Inspection Quality Division
Office for Standards in Education
Alexandra House
33 Kingsway
London WC2B 6SE

Telephone: 020 7421 6800
Website: http://www.ofsted.gov.uk

CONTENTS

---

* Throughout this *Handbook* the term 'pupil' should be taken to include reference where relevant to students in the sixth form.

INTRODUCTION

This Handbook *is published by Her Majesty's Chief Inspector of Schools in England (HMCI) for use by inspectors of secondary schools. Like earlier editions, the* Handbook *will also prove useful for school self-evaluation.*

The *Handbook* has been fully revised. It incorporates the requirements of the differentiated inspection system, in which the most effective schools are offered less intensive inspections than the rest. Both types of inspection lead to summary reports for parents, written to the same standard format, which form part of the longer reports.

The *Handbook* has three parts:

Part 1. Guidance on using the *Evaluation Schedule*
This presents the schedule for evaluating school effectiveness, which contains criteria or benchmarks against which schools can be gauged, together with guidance on collecting and weighing evidence to arrive at judgements.

Part 2. Guidance for inspectors on conducting inspections and writing reports

Part 3. Using the *Handbook* for school self-evaluation

INSPECTION

The *Handbook* shows how the inspection Framework, *Inspecting Schools*, should be applied in the inspection of secondary and middle-deemed secondary schools. The central principles for recognising and judging the quality and standards of schools apply broadly to schools of all types and sizes.

The guidance in this *Handbook* is intended to help ensure that the inspection process is of the highest quality and that judgements about a school are both fair and rigorous. A good inspection is one where:

■ judgements about the educational standards achieved at the school and the strengths and weaknesses in teaching and other aspects are secured by sufficient valid and reliable evidence;

■ the main findings, summarised at the front of the inspection report, together with issues which the school should address in order to improve, are clearly identified and reported to the school.

It is equally important that:

■ inspectors establish an effective working relationship with the school based on professionalism, sensitivity and an understanding of the school's concerns and circumstances;

1

- the process of inspection is well planned and effectively managed;

- there are good communications with the school and individual staff, which lead to a clear and shared understanding of what is involved at each stage of the inspection;

- inspectors readily explore issues with staff through professional dialogue;

- feedback to the school, staff and the governing body, both orally and in writing, is clear and comprehensible.

Inspectors should leave the staff and governors feeling that they have gained from their contact with the members of the team, as well as recognising the thoroughness of the evidence base and understanding and respecting the judgements which emerge. Those involved in running the school should feel that the inspection has provided a valuable contribution to their strategy for improvement.

The new system of inspection applies from January 2000.

SHORT AND FULL INSPECTIONS

This *Handbook* describes a differentiated inspection system. The aim is to offer the most effective schools a SHORT INSPECTION. Other schools will have a FULL INSPECTION, which resembles the inspections carried out to the previous Framework. This differentiated inspection system reflects the Government's commitment to less intervention in schools which are more successful.

Similarities and differences

SHORT and FULL INSPECTIONS have many common features. Both must:

- report on the quality of education provided; the educational standards achieved; the efficiency with which the resources available to the school are managed; and the spiritual, moral, social and cultural development of pupils and students at the school;

- result in an inspection report for the appropriate authority for the school and a summary of the report for parents, written to a standard format;

- be conducted by inspection teams led by a registered inspector and including a lay inspector;

- use similar procedures before and after the inspection;

- continue to identify schools requiring special measures or having serious weaknesses, and to report when a school is underachieving.

The differences in the two types of inspection are that:

- only the FULL INSPECTION will lead to detailed reporting of each subject;

- the FULL INSPECTION needs to fulfil the requirements of the whole *Evaluation Schedule*, but the SHORT INSPECTION may omit some parts;

- feedback is offered to every member of staff during or at the end of FULL INSPECTIONS, but is only done as far as is practicable, after lessons, in SHORT INSPECTIONS;

- teachers are provided with a profile of inspectors' judgements on their lessons after FULL, but not SHORT, INSPECTIONS;

- the SHORT INSPECTION will not necessarily cover the work of every teacher.

The purpose and nature of a SHORT INSPECTION

The SHORT INSPECTION provides an educational 'health check' of the school. The inspection samples the school's work rather than inspecting and reporting fully on each subject. In all but the smallest schools, fewer inspectors will spend fewer days in the school than in a FULL INSPECTION. A SHORT INSPECTION usually lasts for two or three days, whereas a typical FULL INSPECTION lasts for up to a week. The team normally consists of between 2 and 5 inspectors rather than involving as many as the 15 or 16 that are required in the FULL INSPECTION of large secondary schools. Although a SHORT INSPECTION will normally endorse the quality and standards of an effective school, it may sometimes find that a school is underachieving, has serious weaknesses or even requires special measures. This will mean that it is likely to be subject to HMI monitoring and/or an early FULL re-inspection. The report from a SHORT INSPECTION will focus selectively on the school's strengths and areas where improvements are needed. SHORT INSPECTIONS should cause less pressure on the school because the number of lessons observed is considerably smaller than in a FULL INSPECTION.

The purpose and nature of a FULL INSPECTION

The FULL INSPECTION provides an evaluation of the entire school. This includes inspection and reporting of the main subjects of the curriculum by inspectors who have specialist knowledge of those subjects. The FULL INSPECTION leads to a report on every aspect of the school listed in the *Evaluation Schedule*.

Part 1 of the *Handbook* provides guidance on using and interpreting the *Schedule*. All inspectors must be familiar with this guidance. Registered inspectors must ensure that members of their teams who carry responsibility for the inspection of particular aspects of the school thoroughly understand and use the guidance that applies to these aspects. The guidance must be interpreted sensibly during an actual inspection; some parts will be more relevant than others to the inspection of a particular school. It is for the registered inspector to judge where the priorities lie and how best to use the time available.

Part 2 of the *Handbook* provides guidance on how to conduct inspections and write reports. The registered inspector must comply with this guidance and ensure that members of the team also observe it.

SCHOOL MONITORING AND SELF-EVALUATION

The criteria in the *Evaluation Schedule* provide a secure basis for school self-evaluation. OFSTED is committed to promoting self-evaluation as a key aspect of the work of schools. Monitoring and evaluation are essential in order to set priorities and decide the action to take to improve the school's quality and raise the achievements of its pupils.

OFSTED has already made three substantial contributions to self-evaluation by:

   i.   publishing *School Evaluation Matters*, which was issued to all schools;

   ii.   preparing annual *Performance and Assessment (PANDA) reports* for all schools;

   iii. developing a pack for training school evaluators.

Part 3 of this *Handbook* provides schools with advice on how to make the best use of the *Evaluation Schedule* for their own evaluation.

PART 1

GUIDANCE ON USING THE *EVALUATION SCHEDULE*

Part 1 provides guidance for all inspectors and school evaluators on the use
of the *Evaluation Schedule* which is set out in the Framework, *Inspecting Schools.*
The *Schedule* helps you to find the answers to a set of eight questions about a school.

THE STRUCTURE OF THE EVALUATION SCHEDULE

The *Schedule* is arranged in a way which both reflects the evaluation sequence and defines the summary of the inspection report (*see Figure 1*). It highlights the distinction between the **standards** achieved by pupils at the school, or outcomes, and the factors which contribute to these outcomes, **provision**, particularly the quality of teaching, and **leadership and management**. In using each section of the *Schedule*, you should have regard for what is achieved by, and provided for, *all* pupils in the school, whatever their age, attainment, gender, background, ethnicity or special educational need.

Figure 1: Structure of the Evaluation Schedule

CONTEXT AND OVERVIEW

1. What sort of school is it?

OUTCOMES

2. How high are standards?

2.1 The school's results and pupils' or students' achievements

2.2 Pupils' attitudes, values and personal development

QUALITY OF PROVISION

3. How well are pupils or students taught?

4. How good are the curricular and other opportunities offered to pupils or students?

5. How well does the school care for its pupils or students?

6. How well does the school work in partnership with parents?

EFFICIENCY AND EFFECTIVENESS OF MANAGEMENT

7. How well is the school led and managed?

ISSUES FOR THE SCHOOL

8. What should the school do to improve further?

CONTEXT AND OVERVIEW

■ *What sort of school is it?* This section describes the school, summarises its quality and standards, outlines strengths and weaknesses and evaluates improvement since the last inspection.

OUTCOMES

■ *How high are standards?* This is covered in one section, with two areas of enquiry.

- Evaluation of *the school's results and achievements* should focus on the school's results; trends in performance; strengths and weaknesses in particular subjects. You should also judge how well the pupils achieve, i.e. whether *these* pupils in *this* school are getting on as well as they should.

- The section on *pupils' attitudes, values and personal development* explores pupils' response to the school: their attitudes, behaviour, personal development and relationships, and their attendance.

QUALITY OF PROVISION

This is covered in four sections, the first of which is particularly important.

■ *How well are pupils or students taught?* This question requires you to look at the quality of teaching and learning. At the heart of the criteria is the extent to which pupils are challenged and engaged in learning, and are learning at the right level.

■ *How good are the curricular and other opportunities offered to pupils or students?* This question is concerned with the quality and range of the curriculum including provision for pupils' spiritual, moral, social and cultural development, and extra-curricular provision including study support.

■ *How well does the school care for its pupils or students?* This question focuses, in SHORT INSPECTIONS, on the active steps taken by the school to ensure pupils' welfare, health and safety, and in FULL INSPECTIONS on the overall assessment, support and guidance arrangements.

■ *How well does the school work in partnership with parents?* This question explores parents' views of the school and the basis for these views and, in FULL INSPECTIONS, the range of parental involvement in, and links with, the school.

EFFICIENCY AND EFFECTIVENESS OF MANAGEMENT

Effective schools invariably have a clear sense of purpose, drive and direction, supported by efficient and effective management and administration.

■ *How well is the school led and managed?* This question covers a range of enquiries into leadership and management, particularly approaches to enhancing the performance of staff and pupils, the role of governors and, in FULL INSPECTIONS, detailed questions about staffing, accommodation and resources.

THE STRUCTURE OF THE GUIDANCE ON USING THE EVALUATION SCHE

Each section of the guidance includes five elements:

■ The page from the *Evaluation Schedule*, as in the Framework, *Inspecting Schools*;

■ *Inspection focus*, which amplifies the main evaluation and reporting requirements, stressing the features on which an evaluation must concentrate;

■ *Making judgements*, which provides guidance on where to pitch your evaluations, drawing from, but not re-stating, the criteria;

■ *Reporting requirements*, which spells out what is expected in the reports of SHORT and FULL INSPECTIONS. The summary of the report follows the same format in both;

■ *Guidance on using the criteria*, which illustrates how the criteria should be interpreted and how the evidence is tested against them. The criteria amount to a set of standards representing good practice. They provide inspectors with a basis for accurate and consistent evaluation and for the identification of strengths and weaknesses. In reaching overall judgements, *all* the relevant criteria should be considered.

You should use the *Guidance on using the criteria* as a source of reference. In using the guidance, you must focus on the central judgements required by the Framework and not pursue such a diverse range of issues that the inspection becomes unmanageable.

When reporting, you should avoid quoting criteria verbatim and should concentrate on the reporting requirements highlighted in the *Evaluation Schedule*. You must draw evidence into the report in order to illustrate or explain judgements, bring the report to life, and capture the individual characteristics of the school.

USING THE *EVALUATION SCHEDULE* ON SHORT AND FULL INSPECTIONS

The *Schedule* maps out the lines of enquiry for the evaluation of schools. In FULL INSPECTIONS, the school must be evaluated and reported on in terms of all elements of the *Schedule*. In SHORT INSPECTIONS, those elements enclosed in a box are not required. The reporting requirements are indicated by a hollow square (□).

1. WHAT SORT OF SCHOOL IS IT?

Inspectors must report on:

☐   the characteristics of the school;

and evaluate and summarise:

☐   the effectiveness of the school, including the value for money it provides;

☐   the main strengths and weaknesses;

☐   the extent to which the school has improved, or not, since the last inspection;

relating their findings to the specific nature of the school and its pupils.

INSPECTION FOCUS

The inspection report for both SMALL and FULL INSPECTIONS must capture, as succinctly as possible, at the beginning of the summary:

- the main features or characteristics that describe the school;

- your overall view of its effectiveness, particularly in terms of its standards and quality of provision, and the value for money it provides.

After these two opening paragraphs, the report must list:

- the strengths and weaknesses of the school, set out as WHAT THE SCHOOL DOES WELL and WHERE THE SCHOOL SHOULD IMPROVE.

After analysing any changes in the school's performance since the last inspection, the report should state:

- the extent to which the school has improved, or not, since its last inspection;

giving reasons for this judgement.

Only the first of these four elements, the characteristics of the school, is known before the inspection. The other three are summative judgements, decided corporately, normally at the final meeting of the inspection team.

MAKING JUDGEMENTS

☐ The characteristics of the school

The report must start by giving the size, type and nature of the school. It should refer accurately to the background and circumstances of pupils as these are salient to the work of the school and inspection findings. Examples might include social advantage or deprivation, ethnicity, special educational needs (SEN) or pupil mobility.

Example 1.1

Extract from the summary of a report on an 11–16 secondary school with diverse intake

Widerview School is a mixed comprehensive school for pupils in the 11–16 age range with 850 pupils on roll. The school is over-subscribed. The school population is generally stable, with only incidental movement of pupils. The proportion of pupils eligible for free school meals (21 per cent) is slightly higher than the national average. About 20 per cent of pupils in the school come from a long-established Bangladeshi community within the town. There are about 180 pupils for whom English is an additional language, with about 20 who are at the early stages of learning English. One hundred and ninety pupils have special educational needs, marginally above the national average, and 20 have statements. Pupils' attainment on entry is broadly in line with national averages.

The following table (*see Figure 2*) alerts you to the main points you need to consider when preparing your *Pre-Inspection Commentary* and planning the opening paragraph, INFORMATION ABOUT THE SCHOOL section, of the inspection report. The questions and prompts will be more relevant to some schools than others. You must use your judgement when deciding what to include in the full report. You should be guided by whether the information you include is relevant to the quality and standards of the school, and whether it is essential for current and prospective parents.

Figure 2: *The characteristics of the school*	
Is it like other schools?	Refer as appropriate to: • number and age range of pupils; • gender of intake and significant gender imbalance; • type; • any attached units, such as language or special educational needs; • extent of over- or under-subscription; • size and nature of post-16 provision.
What is known of pupils' attainment on entry?	Note any: • variations in the attainment of pupils on entry and over time, if known, including attainment levels of students on entry to post-16 courses, where appropriate.
Does it have a specific designation?	Is the school designated, for example as: • a 'centre of excellence' or 'beacon school'; • a technology college; • part of an Education Action Zone (EAZ), 'Excellence in Cities' or other group (*see Annex 4*)?
Where is the school located and to what extent does the intake reflect the school's location?	The school's context in relation to: • the background of its pupils; • whether the school serves its immediate area; • recent patterns of admission and transfer.
What is the proportion of pupils eligible for free schools meals?	Note: • how this compares with levels nationally and with similar types of schools (if known); • any trends with successive intakes.
What different groups are there in the school?	Note the numbers and proportion of: • ethnic groups represented in the school in significant numbers, including refugees and asylum seekers; • Traveller children; • pupils for whom English is an additional language (EAL) and number of EAL pupils who are at the early stages of learning English; • pupils with special educational needs (SEN), especially those with statements; • other identifiable groups, for example non-attending pupils.

☐ The effectiveness of the school

At the end of the inspection you need to summarise the team's view of how good the school is. You should substantiate this judgement, particularly in terms of the *standards* achieved by pupils by the time they leave, the quality of education, particularly *teaching*, and the *leadership and management* of the school. The **overall effectiveness** of the school is reported in the summary of the report, together with a comment on the *value for money* it provides (*see page 15*). Where the school has a sixth form, you should *also* report on the cost-effectiveness of post-16 provision (*see Annex 1 of this Handbook*).

The effectiveness of the school is an overall judgement based on the standards pupils achieve, the quality of education it provides, its leadership and management, and how far it is improving. To reach a judgement about overall effectiveness, you will need to weigh up carefully the team's conclusions about the following indicators of effectiveness:

■ how well pupils achieve, and their attitudes, values and personal development;

■ the quality of education provided, particularly teaching;

■ how well the school is led and managed;

■ how far the school has improved or maintained very high standards since the last inspection.

In coming to your conclusions, you will need to take account of the characteristics of the school and the background of its pupils. You may find it helpful to collect together the team's corporate judgements that you have recorded in the *Record of Corporate Judgements* and place them on a table such as that shown below. You need to give due weight to each area, giving particular attention to how well pupils achieve.

Figure 3: Aid to judging effectiveness

Judgement recording grade		1	2	3	4	5	6	7	
STANDARDS Pupils' achievements are:	Excellent	★	★	★	★	★	★	★	Very poor
Attitudes, values and personal development are:	Excellent	★	★	★	★	★	★	★	Very poor
PROVISION The quality of education, particularly teaching, is:	Excellent	★	★	★	★	★	★	★	Very poor
LEADERSHIP AND MANAGEMENT Leadership and management are:	Excellent	★	★	★	★	★	★	★	Very poor
IMPROVEMENT Improvement or maintenance of very high standards is:	Excellent	★	★	★	★	★	★	★	Very poor
CONTEXTUAL FACTORS The context of school in the local environment is:	Very unfavourable	★	★	★	★	★	★	★	Very favourable
EFFECTIVENESS The overall effectiveness of the school is:	Excellent	★	★	★	★	★	★	★	Very poor

The following characteristics illustrate where to pitch judgements about the effectiveness of the school.

Very good or excellent	The school achieves the highest standards possible in most of its work. High proportions of pupils are keen to learn. There are few problems of behaviour or absenteeism. The teaching is consistently good, with much that is very good; and virtually all pupils progress very well. The staff constantly look for ways to improve the quality of their teaching, are imaginative and make challenging demands of pupils. There are very good arrangements to support all pupils and care for them and the school has a strong partnership with parents and carers. The school is well governed and self-critical. It knows what it does well, where its weaknesses are and how to improve them. It has made a significant improvement since its last inspection or has sustained high standards. It provides good or very good value for money.
Satisfactory or better	The school achieves standards that are at least as good as they should be. Pupils have good attitudes and are able to express themselves clearly. Almost all the teaching is at least satisfactory and much is good or better, and pupils are learning well. The school has developed a curriculum that meets the needs of individual pupils and provides opportunities which benefit all pupils. There are sound care and guidance arrangements and the school keeps parents and carers informed about their son or daughter's progress and enlists their support. The school has made satisfactory improvement since its last inspection and responds adequately to the challenges or issues it faces. It is inclusive in its policies, outlook and practices, and is led and managed so that all these measures are achieved in a cost-effective way, providing satisfactory value for money.

However, if the judgement is that the school is **not as effective as it should be, poor or very poor**, then you must consider as a team:

- whether or not the **school is failing, or likely to fail, to give its pupils an acceptable standard of education, and thus requires special measures;**

- whether or not **the school, although providing an acceptable standard of education, nevertheless has serious weaknesses in one or more areas of its work;**

- whether **the school, although not identified as having serious weakness, is judged to be under-achieving.**

Any of these findings must always be *stated explicitly in the report* using the form of words highlighted above (*see Annex 2*).

Example 1.2

Extract from a summary report on a large secondary school

This is a successful school which achieves very high standards and has many strengths. There is only a sprinkling of minor weaknesses, mainly too narrow a range of teaching methods in some lessons. Leadership inspires both students and staff to do well. The school is very well organised and managed, and gives good value for money.

[Overall: a very good school (2)]

Judging value for money

The value for money provided by the school is a composite assessment of its effectiveness and efficiency in relation to its costs. You can only make this judgement when you have considered all the other elements of the inspection.

Your judgements should be based on a careful weighing up of the team's conclusions about:

■ the overall effectiveness of the school;

taking into account the characteristics of the school and the background of its pupils. You should then relate these evaluations to:

■ the unit costs of the school and its cost-effectiveness;

taking account of the efficiency with which the school is run.

In broad terms, you should consider value for money as effectiveness set against costs, and this can be illustrated in a two-way table.

Figure 4: Value for money as effectiveness set against cost

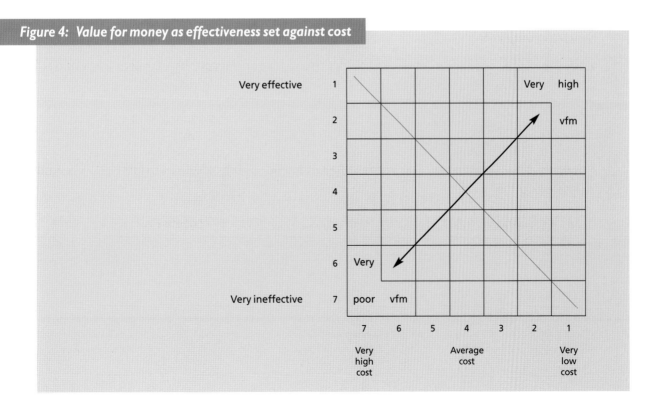

15

Put another way, you should consider the main judgement recording statement for the overall effectiveness of the school alongside contextual factors and the school's expenditure per pupil.

Judgement recording grade		1	2	3	4	5	6	7	
EFFECTIVENESS The overall effectiveness of the school:	Excellent	★	★	★	★	★	★	★	Very poor
CONTEXTUAL FACTORS The school and its pupils in the local environment:	Very favourable	★	★	★	★	★	★	★	Very unfavourable
UNIT COSTS The school's expenditure per pupil:	Very low	★	★	★	★	★	★	★	Very high
VALUE FOR MONEY The value for money provided by the school:	Excellent	★	★	★	★	★	★	★	Very poor

☐ The main strengths and weaknesses of the school

At its final meeting, the team must corporately decide which aspects of the school are particularly good and which aspects are weak, if any. These should be recorded in the sections of the inspection report headed:

WHAT THE SCHOOL DOES WELL

and

WHAT COULD BE IMPROVED

The balance between these strengths and areas for improvement should reflect the overall quality of the school. The areas for improvement should form the basis for the issues for action to improve standards and quality, set out in section 8 of the *Evaluation Schedule*, WHAT SHOULD THE SCHOOL DO TO IMPROVE FURTHER?

☐ The extent to which the school has improved, or not, since the last inspection

Your evaluation of the school's current performance and your analysis of how the school has changed since its last inspection are integral to your judgements about its improvement. By the end of the inspection you must be able to report on how much improvement has been brought about and judge whether it has been enough. This overall judgement must relate to:

- how much change could reasonably be expected;

- what the school has done and whether it has been enough.

You must give reasons for the overall judgement, drawing on illustrative evidence from different sections of the report. This should normally include, for example:

- trends in attainment across subjects and whether the school is on course to meet or exceed its targets;

- improvements in the quality of teaching and pupils' learning;

- how well the school's leadership has responded to the previous inspection, and what it has done to improve or maintain high standards and balance the costs and effectiveness of its provision.

How much change could reasonably be expected?

The previous report indicated what improvements were needed. The school may also have identified its own areas for improvement. You will need to consider the improvement made in terms of national trends in performance and the school's own targets, and any changes in the characteristics of the pupils and students who attend the school. Some schools will have done well to maintain very high standards or sustain the quality of what they provide. For all schools there is an expectation of either continued improvement or sustained excellence.

In FULL INSPECTIONS, each section of the commentary and each subject report should refer to improvement in the areas or subjects concerned, as applicable. In particular, you should consider standards, teaching, and leadership and management, as well as the school's ethos, in making your judgement.

The threshold for **expected** ('satisfactory') **improvement** is illustrated by the presence of all or most of the following features:

In terms of the **standards achieved**, there is evidence of:

- substantial improvement in attendance, attitudes and behaviour of pupils, if these had been poor or unsatisfactory;

- improved results in relation to national averages such that:
  - schools with low standards have improved more than the national average;
  - schools with average standards have kept pace with national trends;
  - high-performing schools have sustained high standards;
  - there are noticeable improvements in core subjects;

- improvement in relation to similar schools, such that:
  - schools which have had low performance reach the average;
  - schools which did relatively well sustain that position.

Schools whose performance, despite some improvement, still remains below the great majority of similar schools are unlikely to merit the 'satisfactory' judgement.

In terms of the **quality of education provided**, there is evidence of:

- improved teaching in the areas where it was weakest;

- a successful effort to consider and redress other areas of weakness identified in the previous report;

- effective action on the main key issues, particularly those related to standards;

- clear efforts by the school to monitor its progress.

In **leadership and management**, there is evidence of:

- reported weaknesses having been overcome;

- resources and expertise being directed towards priorities related to raising standards;

- development of self-evaluation.

In relation to the **ethos** of the school, there is:

- general staff commitment to the achievement of high standards;

- satisfaction with the school by pupils and parents;

- good working relationships across the school.

What the school has done and whether it has been enough?

In making this judgement you will need to give greatest weight to any changes in the standards achieved by pupils, the quality of teaching, leadership and how the school is managed. The weighting you give to other changes will depend on the impact they have on the standards achieved.

Illustrate your judgement to show how change has been brought about. Reasons for change might include:

- effective action planning;

- the appointment of a new headteacher or other key staff;

- the school's ability to identify and deal effectively with its own weaknesses.

A governing body is not obliged to address a key issue, but where it has not, it should have a convincing reason.

If you decide that the improvement has not been good enough, you will need to consider whether the school has serious weaknesses in one or more areas, or requires special measures to help it to improve.

How well is the school placed to continue to improve?

In your judgement of leadership and management you will have assessed the school's commitment to improvement. The overall judgement about how much the school has improved since the last inspection must be consistent with this.

Example 1.3

School improvement

The school has made significant improvement since the last inspection (1996). The percentages of pupils reaching Levels 5 and 6 in national tests in English, mathematics and science at Key Stage 3 are now virtually the same as the national figures. This represents a positive gain. Similarly, the percentage of pupils achieving five A*–C grades (42 per cent) and five A*–G grades (94 per cent) have both improved by about 15 per cent and are now nearly at national average levels. No unsatisfactory teaching was observed during the inspection, which also represents a considerable improvement on the figure of 14 per cent in the previous report in 1996. This reflects well on the effectiveness of the leadership of the school in its drive to improve teaching, outlined in the action plan.

[Overall: very good improvement (2)]

Example 1.4 illustrates how the first five sections of a summary report might appear when completed in the way described in this section.

Example 1.4 Summary of the inspection report

FIRS DENE SCHOOL
Longton
Headteacher: Jack Hilton
Date of inspection: 23–25 March 2000

The school was inspected by five inspectors, led by Robert Talent. This is a summary of the full inspection report, which is available from the school.

INFORMATION ABOUT THE SCHOOL

Firs Dene is a large comprehensive secondary school of 1,350 boys and girls aged 11–18, with 248 students in the sixth form. The attainment of pupils on entry to the school at age 11 is average overall. Two hundred and six pupils have special educational needs, a proportion broadly in line with the national average. Fewer than 1 per cent of pupils are from minority ethnic backgrounds and 11 pupils have English as an additional language. Eighty pupils are entitled to free school meals, well below the national average.

HOW GOOD THE SCHOOL IS

This is a good and effective school which is heavily over-subscribed. Through strong leadership and a clear commitment to school improvement it provides a very good quality of teaching. Governors and school staff create a very positive climate for learning which ensures that high standards are achieved by pupils, particularly in the sixth form. The school provides good value for money, and provision for the vibrant sixth form is unusually cost-effective.

WHAT THE SCHOOL DOES WELL

- Most pupils achieve high standards of attainment at Key Stage 3 and Key Stage 4, and many sixth form students achieve very high standards, placing the school in the highest 5 per cent nationally
- Very good teaching provides high expectations and stimulating challenges for pupils
- Pupils respond very well to the dynamic teaching and very positive climate for learning sustained in classrooms
- There is a well-established culture of school improvement, through regular monitoring and self-evaluation, which ensures continuing improvements to teaching and contributes to pupils' high standards
- There is strong and effective leadership and management from the governors, headteacher and senior staff of the school

WHAT COULD BE IMPROVED

- The motivation and attainment of some lower attaining pupils in Key Stage 3 in art, music and drama
- The teaching of information and communications technology in Key Stage 4 so that it fully meets National Curriculum requirements
- Opportunities for pupils' spiritual development and the provision of religious education for all in the sixth form

The areas for improvement will form the basis of the governors' action plan.

HOW THE SCHOOL HAS IMPROVED SINCE ITS LAST INSPECTION

Firs Dene has succeeded in extending its already high standards since the last inspection in March 1996. Further improvements in teaching have ensured that levels of attainment have risen significantly in each Key Stage, and dramatically so in the sixth form. The school has responded very effectively to the four key issues identified: to improve careers education, aspects of pupils' personal and social education, the teaching of information and communications technology at Key Stage 3, and provision for pupils with special educational needs. The effectiveness of the school's response underscores its commitment to continue to improve further.

2. HOW HIGH ARE STANDARDS?

2.1 THE SCHOOL'S RESULTS AND PUPILS' OR STUDENTS' ACHIEVEMENTS

Inspectors must *interpret* and report on:

- [ ] the school's results and other performance data for all subjects at the end of each stage of education, particularly in English, mathematics and science, highlighting any variations of achievement by different groups of pupils and students and in different subjects;

- [ ] trends in results over time;

- [ ] the school's progress towards its targets, including comment on whether the targets are sufficiently challenging.

Inspectors must *evaluate* and report on:

- [ ] standards of work seen, emphasising literacy and numeracy, and highlighting strengths and weaknesses in what pupils and students know, understand and can do;

> - all the subjects inspected, focusing on the work of the oldest pupils at each stage;
> - the variations between different groups of pupils and between subjects;

- [ ] how well pupils achieve, taking account of the progress they have made, the level of demand placed on them and other relevant factors.

In determining their judgements, inspectors should consider, where relevant, the extent to which:

- the results in National Curriculum and other tests, examinations and accreditations match or exceed the average for all schools;

- the school is either maintaining very high standards or improving as expected;

- the school sets challenging targets and is on course to meet or exceed them;

- pupils with special educational needs, having English as an additional language or who are gifted and talented, are making good progress;

- standards are consistently high across subjects;

- there are no significant differences in the standards achieved by pupils of different gender or ethnic background;

- results in the school are high compared with those of similar schools (or show significant added value in relation to pupils' earlier results);

- pupils' achievements meet or exceed the levels set by: the National Curriculum and, where applicable, the local agreed syllabus for religious education; and any examination or assessment objectives.

INSPECTION FOCUS

The inspection report must give a clear and unequivocal interpretation of the school's results and how well pupils and students are achieving, giving reasons for these findings. Parents and others who read the report need an informed guide to the school's results: what they say about the school, how they should be interpreted, and how inspectors regard the achievements of pupils.

In this guidance we use the term *standards* to denote the educational attainment of pupils in relation to some clear benchmark, such as National Curriculum levels, or descriptions, at the end of a Key Stage. 'High standards', for example, means that a higher proportion of pupils of a particular age are succeeding at or beyond the level set than in the majority of schools. We also use standards in connection with other less measurable but broadly understood characteristics such as attitudes and behaviour.

Achievement, on the other hand, reflects the accomplishments of pupils in relation to what you would expect of those particular pupils. There are few clear reference points. Reference to terms such as 'ability' or 'aptitude' requires caution, for it is questionable what evidence you will have of such attributes. Prior attainment is a more secure reference point, if it has been measured, but essentially you should judge achievement by applying insight and expertise to all the evidence you have about the pupils, taking account of what they know, understand and can do, and what they are being asked to do. Broader indicators, such as measures which compare standards with those in similar schools and value-added measures, are also helpful in indicating the relative progress of pupils and providing a clue to how well they are achieving.

To judge standards you will have two main strategies. The *first* is to analyse the school's performance data before the inspection begins in order to determine the pattern of results in English, mathematics and science at Key Stage 3 and in all subjects and courses at 16, 17 and 18 years, where appropriate. The data will also help you to judge whether the results are good enough when compared to all schools and those in similar circumstances, and indicate trends in performance over several years. This analysis should give an indication of some of the school's strengths and weaknesses and provide you with a starting point for the inspection.

The *second*, equally important, strategy once you are in the school, is to find out for yourself what pupils know, understand and can do and how well they are achieving. Firsthand inspection evidence gives you the current picture of what pupils, including different groups of pupils, are doing well or not so well, and how effectively they are learning. **Your findings should be linked, through other parts of the report, with your diagnosis of what the school is doing to maximise pupils' achievement, particularly in terms of the quality of teaching. If there are differences between the performance data and what you see during the inspection, you should state these clearly and advance the likely reason(s).**

You should give the sixth form equivalent emphasis to other key stages in reporting on examination results, vocational qualifications and the standards of work in lessons. You should make separate evaluations of standards in advanced level courses (GCE, AS and A level courses, advanced GNVQ and other two-year vocational courses) and in one-year intermediate or foundation level GNVQ courses. You should also comment on the development of key skills which may be being taught for a separate qualification.

MAKING JUDGEMENTS

Before any inspection, you should analyse performance data printed in the *PICSI report* and any obtained from the school. The data will give you a picture of:

- the school's results in tests, examinations and other forms of accreditation;

- how the school's results relate to national averages and how they compare with similar schools;

- how the results have changed in recent years;

- other features of the school and the pupils it serves.

The *PICSI report* indicates, for example, whether results range from well above average, or very high, to very low, compared with all schools. The *PICSI report* also offers comparisons with similar schools. Gradings attached to these findings replicate *PICSI* grades A* (or 1) to E* (or 7). In all cases, you must decide whether the standards of the school are satisfactory or not.

You may encounter schools with high, or very high, standards, which are nevertheless not high enough in some or all subjects, or for all groups of pupils. Here, reporting in terms such as 'the school achieves very good results in English and science, but attainment in mathematics, while above average, is not as high as it should be/not sufficiently high/too low' begins to make the link. You may find a school in which all results are 'well above average', but lack of success at the highest levels and/or the indifferent progress made from a high-achieving early stage may lead you to conclude that the results, while being well above average, are too low for the pupils concerned. In an underachieving school the *PICSI report* may reveal grades A or B for national comparisons and D or E for like school comparisons.

Performance data, however, do not tell the whole story about a school's standards. They relate to the past, not the present. The school may have undertaken monitoring by ethnicity, for example, or developed value-added measures which can inform your analysis. Your judgements therefore need to take account of all relevant evidence.

During the inspection, you can supplement and update your view of standards by:

- analysing the school's targets and the basis on which they have been set;

- identifying strengths and weaknesses in attainment in the subjects of the curriculum, judged by observations of lessons, discussion with pupils and analysis of the work they have completed and assessments made;

- reaching a view of how well pupils achieve on the basis of their earlier achievements, the work they are doing and the demands made on them.

Your evaluation of standards must pay particular attention to pupils' **competence in literacy and numeracy,** drawing on evidence across the curriculum. You will need to consider whether pupils' skills in these areas are well enough developed to ensure they have full access to the curriculum or whether their skills are too low and are a barrier to learning. In FULL INSPECTIONS, you are required to report your judgements on all the subjects you inspect. The standards achieved in subjects must be referenced to the expected levels for the oldest pupils or students at each Key Stage, in the years when they become 14, 16 and 18. Refer to the destinations of leavers at 16, 17 and 18 years if known (*see Example 2.1.1*).

Example 2.1.1

Extract from an inspection report of a secondary school

In 1998, pupils' results in National Curriculum tests at the end of Key Stage 3, at the age of 14, were well above the national comparison with all schools in English and mathematics and were close to the national average in science. In English and in mathematics the percentage of pupils reaching Level 6 was well above average. Work of an equally high standard was seen in the work of the more able pupils in history, art, music, and design and technology. Most average-attaining pupils were achieving in line with National Curriculum levels expected in English and mathematics. The work in science and modern foreign languages was a strength with these groups, with a high proportion of pupils (over 90 per cent) reaching the expected levels.

Pupils achieve high standards in public examinations at the age of 16. Over the last three years pupils have achieved well above average results, with a rising trend of success, at a much faster rate than that nationally. In the 1998 results there were particular strengths in English, mathematics, business studies and geography, and rises in results in French, German, and design and technology. Only in art and design and drama were results below the national average for A*–C grades. Results were good on GNVQ courses at Key Stage 4, with all pupils gaining the Part 1 Intermediate and three-quarters of candidates the Foundation qualification. The performance of boys in Key Stage 4 reflects the national picture and lags behind that of girls. Standards attained, in lessons seen during the inspection, confirm and substantiate the picture given by examination results. Levels of work in English, mathematics and geography were high, with some particularly good work by the more able pupils. Standards in the drama GCSE group were not good enough, with weaknesses in understanding of dramatic texts and in the capacity of pupils to co-ordinate and structure a piece of their own devising.

Students' attainment in GCE Advanced level courses has been very high for several years. This reflects consistent and very high value being achieved by the school as the students moved from examination at 16 to examination at 18. There is a significantly higher proportion of the top grades A and B achieved by students than is found nationally, in 1998, in mathematics, biology, English and French. Inspection evidence confirmed these standards with work of high challenge and very good levels of understanding and skill in mathematics, English, French, biology and history.

[Overall: very high standards (2)]

Always explain in the summary if your judgements on the basis of firsthand inspection evidence differ in some way from your interpretation of the data about subjects. Detailed explanation is best given in the relevant subject section in the report of a FULL INSPECTION.

Example 2.1.2

Explanation of differing judgements

Examination results in English in GCSE in 1998 were below the national average for grades A*–C (38 per cent compared with 45 per cent nationally) with no A grades achieved. However, the response by the English department to these figures has been immediate and effective. In Years 10 and 11, specific, well-structured approaches to reading non-fiction texts have been prepared and taught and the evidence of inspection shows thoughtful and analytic understanding by pupils, based on a much clearer sense of how non-fiction texts are constructed. Pupils have developed confident and effective skills in establishing the nature of argument and the way it is sustained in written material, and are able to identify and explain the features of the text in their answers. Many of the more able pupils were showing high degrees of understanding, both in classroom answers and in their written work. Average and below-average pupils were also showing marked improvement in their performance. The inspection evidence showed work at more demanding levels than previously.

When judging how well pupils achieve, use as your starting point the grade provided in the *PICSI report* which compares the school's performance with similar schools and any value-added data, but your main evidence comprises your judgements of attainment and progress, pupils' work and the demands posed by the teaching.

The following characteristics illustrate where to pitch your judgements about results and *how well pupils achieve* in secondary schools.

	Results	Achievements
Very high or excellent	Results are well above average or almost all pupils are on course to meet or exceed expected standards in English, mathematics and science by 14 and 16 and standards appropriate to the course at post-16. Standards of literacy and numeracy are very high.	Most pupils are working at or near their capacity and achieving well in terms of: earlier attainment; value-added measures and comparisons with similar schools.
Satisfactory or better	Results are at least average, compared with all other schools and current work indicates standards are rising. Standards in literacy and numeracy are adequate for work in other subjects. Standards in other subjects of the National Curriculum are in line with expectations for pupils of the particular age.	Pupils are making satisfactory progress and achieving as much as could be expected, some of them more. The school is achieving at least as well as most similar schools.

However standards (results and/or achievement) are **unlikely to be satisfactory** if any of the following are present:

- the school's standards are low in relation to those of similar schools;

- there is evidence of low achievement in English, mathematics and science in the school;

- the trend of improvement in test results is lower than the national rate (unless the results are already high);

- there is evidence of widespread underachievement or by particular groups of pupils, such as boys, girls, gifted and talented pupils, minority ethnic pupils or pupils with special educational needs;

- pupils' skills in literacy and numeracy are too low to cope with the current curriculum and do not adequately prepare them for the next stages of education or employment.

Example 2.1.3

Unsatisfactory standards in a school requiring special measures

Standards in the school are unsatisfactory with serious concerns about underachievement by many groups of pupils who show themselves capable of learning much more. The most able pupils in Year 10 are significantly below the standards expected in English, science, history and RE. There are serious weaknesses in average and below-average pupils' literacy skills in Year 10, which means they fail to cope adequately with the range of reading the curriculum requires, with particular problems in science and geography, where technical and specialist language is frequently beyond them. The school's Key Stage 3 National Curriculum tests results have declined steadily over the last three years, with very poor performances by girls in mathematics, contrary to national trends.

[Overall: very low standards (7)]

In all cases make sure you give reasons for your judgements and link this judgement with what you are finding in other aspects of the inspection, so that you provide a consistent message throughout the report. For example, if teaching throughout the school is satisfactory or better, yet the school's standards are too low, you must explain these apparently conflicting findings in clear and convincing terms (*see Example 2.1.4*).

Example 2.1.4

Conflicting findings: satisfactory teaching in a school where standards are low

The school has tackled the key issues of the weaknesses in its teaching, as found in the previous report. The policies of much closer monitoring and evaluation, together with a constructive mentor system, have raised the quality of teaching, particularly in the match of work to pupils and the range of methods used. At the same time a successful and firmly implemented behaviour policy has improved the classroom atmosphere. Standards are still too low but show encouraging signs of moving in the right direction.

Example 2.1.5

School identifying weakness between subjects: extract from an English inspector's Notebook

Issue:

Why are KS3 English scores only in line with national averages, when mathematics and science are significantly above?

Discussion with HoD English:

She recognises situation and is concerned. Has planned much stronger focus on reading and understanding in Y7 and Y8 and extending a vocabulary for literacy and critical understanding in Y9. New materials evident in departmental scheme of work. Further work on extending range of writing [EF10].

Inspection evidence:

Reading for accuracy and understanding good in all years at KS3 [see EFs 3, 5, 13, 14].

REPORTING REQUIREMENTS

SUMMARY REPORT	On all inspections you must complete the table headed STANDARDS and provide a summary judgement about pupils' attainment in relation to the particular strengths and weaknesses in the standards of work seen and how well pupils or students achieve. You must provide brief evaluations about the strengths and weaknesses of the school's results, trends over time, targets, standards of work seen, and how well pupils achieve.
	If any of these are a feature of improvement in the school, record this in the section HOW THE SCHOOL HAS IMPROVED SINCE ITS LAST INSPECTION.
	Any subjects or areas of work that are particularly good or need to improve must be reported on under WHAT THE SCHOOL DOES WELL or WHAT COULD BE IMPROVED.
SHORT INSPECTIONS	Expand in the commentary any items featured in WHAT THE SCHOOL DOES WELL or WHAT COULD BE IMPROVED. Complete the data tables at the back of the report.
FULL INSPECTIONS	Report fully under the section headed HOW HIGH ARE STANDARDS? Complete the data tables at the back of the report.

☐ The school's results and other performance data

Do the school's results in National Curriculum and other tests match or exceed the average for all schools? To what extent do pupils' achievements meet or exceed the levels set by the National Curriculum the local agreed syllabus for religious education and any assessment objectives?

Using the information from the *PICSI report*, find out how well pupils have performed **in relation to all schools**. The letter grade, signifying this performance, must be reported in the summary report. Remember that this grade represents overall standards and that it may mask some important variations between subjects or groups of pupils. Look also at data provided in the *PICSI report* which show the proportion of pupils in the year group that achieved different levels in each subject. Note carefully how the school's distribution of results **compares with the proportions for all schools** for each stage and how the distribution of results compares **with similar schools**. This must also be reported in the summary report by a letter grade unless exceptional circumstances exist in which reporting the grade would give an unfair picture of the school.

In these circumstances, the team has discretion to change the comparative grade by one grade. Before making such a change, the team should consider carefully the evidence available to support a change of grade, taking particular note of any proper value-added information available. If it is considered that a change of more than one grade is needed, then OFSTED must be informed and the supporting evidence submitted.

You should examine the information in the *PICSI report* to find out:

■ how well pupils attained in English, mathematics and science at 14 and 16 years;

■ how well pupils attained in one subject compared with another at 16;

■ how well boys' attainment compared with girls' in relation to national averages;

■ how well students performed post-16.

Discuss with the headteacher of schools serving more than one significant ethnic minority group any other significant variation in attainment by different groups of pupils.

Before the inspection, make sure you understand, in detail, the characteristics of the school. Take full account of the information in *Forms S1* and *S2* as they provide important details about the pupils. You need to do this in preparation for interpreting the data. You should be aware of the extent to which small numbers of pupils reduce the confidence you can have in results as an indicator of performance. You should consider if **high pupil mobility** affects the picture of the school's performance by asking for evidence of such pupils' attainment on entry to the school. Take account of the Key Stage 2 results of incoming pupils.

In those sixth forms which operate collaboratively with other institutions in the provision of post-16 courses, some of the students' results will be a consequence of teaching elsewhere. You should take account of this when commenting on results, particularly where there is a marked disparity between some subjects or courses. If the sixth form is part of a consortium, you may find it helpful to consider the school's examination results alongside those for the consortium as a whole. If there is high pupil mobility ask the school for evidence of such pupils' attainment when they enter the school, and judge what effect if any, this has on the school's performance.

Example 2.1.6

Pre-Inspection Commentary

In 1998 the school's GCSE results of 61 per cent of pupils gaining five or more A*–C grades were well above the national average of 44.4 per cent. The proportion of pupils gaining five or more A*–G grades (90 per cent) was close to the national average of 89.6 per cent. In both categories the school's results were above the national average over the past three years, with girls attaining higher results than boys, as in the national picture, but there may be an issue with some girls underachieving or not entered. In this year and over the past three years pupils' results have been well above the national average, with the average points score showing a rising trend, at a much faster rate than the national average. In comparison with similar schools the school's GCSE points score is average and is much lower than similar schools for pupils obtaining one A*–G grade, but the school provides vocational courses for some pupils aged 14–16.

The four-year GCSE trend has been:
1995	*50 per cent*	*five A*–C*
1996	*53 per cent*	
1997	*47 per cent*	
1998	*61 per cent*	*44.0 average points*

The four-year 2+AL trend has been:
1995	*17.5*
1996	*23.6*
1997	*23.3*
1998	*24.4 average points score*

School documentation:

Forms refer to the 18 per cent of pupils on roll who experience turbulence in their schooling, gaining proportionately fewer exam successes and appearing to underachieve. HT notes that attainment on entry has regressed from slightly above to below average in VRQ scores over the past two years (102.9 to 95.6 in five years). KS2 NC average level on entry is now around 3.7.

Parents' views:

Very positive responses on standards and expectations from most comments at the parents' meeting. Questionnaires recorded 96 per cent satisfied or better with progress made by their children, 95 per cent satisfied or better with expectations that they work hard to achieve their best, of 150 returns.

Issues for the inspection:

- *Why are some girls underachieving?*
- *Why do a significant proportion of pupils appear not to complete GNVQ courses?*
- *What accounts for the relatively weak performance of DR and A&D and the improvement this year of MFL?*
- *What impact is target-setting having on standards?*
- *Check whether lower-attainers are getting a fair deal.*
- *What is the effect of pupil mobility?*

☐ Trends in results over time

Is the school either maintaining very high standards or improving as expected?

You should examine any performance **trends**, for example:

- how well the school has improved **compared with all schools**;

- whether the performance in any **subject** is persistently lower than in others;

- whether the performance of **girls in relation to boys** is different from that found nationally;

- any significant variation in performance by **particular groups of pupils**.

See if results of teacher assessments are broadly in line with the results of National Curriculum tests. Discrepancies may indicate important factors such as low expectation or over-grading. Once you have assessed all the data pose some questions and begin to make some hypotheses about the school's performance.

When you visit the school before the inspection, ask how the school analyses its results, to identify strengths and weaknesses and whether it monitors the results of pupils from minority ethnic backgrounds and any other group; check what action it is taking in the light of this evidence. Find out about any pupils in the year group who were not assessed by teachers, or who did not take National Curriculum tests. If there were many absences you need to take this into account in interpreting the data.

☐ The school's progress towards its targets

Does the school set challenging targets and is it on course to meet or exceed them?

Evaluate how well the school collates and presents its results and other performance data so that they can be understood easily by those concerned, for example parents and governors. Find out if the school has analysed all its data to set targets, and used it to take action to make any necessary improvements.

Look for evidence that the school has identified any specific weaknesses within or between subjects, or that particular groups of pupils perform relatively less well than others.

The governing body, with the headteacher, will have agreed targets with the LEA to raise standards in English and mathematics. Many schools will also have set targets in other areas of the curriculum and for particular pupils and groups. To judge whether the targets are appropriate, you should evaluate the extent to which the school has:

- used its performance data to see how it compares with similar schools;

- formed an accurate appraisal of the extent to which any pupils are underachieving;

- identified the strengths, and particularly any weaknesses in teaching and learning in the core subjects and taken action to improve weaknesses;

- analysed its performance data in detail to see which aspects of subjects need most improvement;

- assessed the need for targets in non-academic areas such as behaviour;

- set aspirational targets which in your view should nevertheless be just achievable.

Pay particular attention to the school's or LEA's analysis of data to find out differences in the **performance by different groups of pupils,** for example:

- boys compared with girls;

- pupils from minority ethnic backgrounds;

- gifted and talented pupils.

Look for evidence of whether the school has identified particular groups of pupils that are performing relatively less well than others.

Example 2.1.7

Challenging targets

In 1998, the school analysed its GCSE results and found that the five A*–C figure was below national averages. They felt that boys were underachieving particularly and focused on pupils at the D/C GCSE boundary, as estimated by teachers in English, mathematics and science, at the start of Year 11 (September 1998). Of 40 pupils in this category (27 boys, 13 girls) the target was to gain C grades in English, mathematics and science for 60 per cent (25 pupils). In summer 1999, 31 out of the targeted pupils achieved C grades in all of the three subjects, a very good outcome.

☐ Standards of work seen

In SHORT INSPECTIONS, inspectors should judge attainment in lessons wherever they are confident of doing so competently and always in the core subjects of English, mathematics and science.

In FULL INSPECTIONS only, you will need to undertake a more detailed evaluation of:

- standards in subjects and courses inspected, focusing on the work of the oldest pupils and students in each key stage;

- variations between the standards of different groups of pupils and between different subjects or courses.

Are standards consistently high across subjects?

During the inspection, evaluate standards by reference to **the expected levels set by the National Curriculum or requirements of GCSE, GCE examinations and vocational courses.** In SHORT INSPECTIONS, make sure you have enough evidence to report on what pupils do well or not so well. Look for any examples of outstanding achievement, say in art, music or physical education. Also look out for clear gaps in pupils' knowledge, understanding or skills.

In FULL INSPECTIONS, make sure you have sufficient evidence to evaluate standards in English, mathematics, science, and information technology **in relation to the expected levels** and in RE (where it is inspected) **in relation to the locally agreed syllabus.** Concentrate on the **oldest pupils at the end of each key stage.**

In all inspections you should plan the best way of securing the evidence you need to evaluate standards. You need to do this in liaison with the school. The quantity of the evidence is much less on SHORT INSPECTIONS so you must identify what needs to be done at the pre-inspection stage to make sure you capture essential evidence.

Gather evidence by:

■ observing and talking to pupils in lessons;

■ listening to pupils asking and answering questions in plenary sessions;

■ analysing the work they have produced;

■ looking at records of attainment;

■ questioning and talking to groups of pupils;

■ talking to co-ordinators and looking at records together;

■ looking at course work.

When you evaluate standards of literacy and numeracy, find out how well pupils use their skills in other subjects, or whether their understanding of important aspects of these subjects is hindered by poor literacy and/or numeracy skills.

On *Evidence Forms*, make sure that you record pupils' strengths and weaknesses within and between subjects so that you can accumulate a picture of the school's performance.

Bring all of your evidence together so that you can make an overall judgement. You will need to estimate the proportion of pupils who are on course to **achieve or exceed the expected levels in the National Curriculum at 14 and results at 16, and how results compare with national figures at 18.** Then you are in a position to judge how high standards are.

You should compare your judgements on standards in the core subjects with the results of end of Key Stage tests or other assessment data. If there are differences between your findings and the data, you should explain why this is so.

Are pupils with special educational needs, those with English as an additional language or who are gifted or talented, making good progress? Are there significant differences in the standards achieved by pupils of different gender or ethnic backgrounds?

Throughout both SHORT and FULL INSPECTIONS you should make sure you focus on how well different groups of pupils are performing. Start with any assessment data the school has to guide your observations. If the school cannot provide any analysis of data, make sure you check in lessons and from pupils' work how well different groups are doing. If your observation of pupils' work leads you to suspect that a particular group of pupils is achieving at a relatively higher or lower level, gather sufficient evidence of what pupils know, understand and can do to substantiate and exemplify your judgements. Since SHORT INSPECTIONS are designated for the most effective schools, such schools may have a clear view, supported by evidence, of the performance of different groups. This should make your task easier. But check the school's view by focusing in particular on such pupils.

In FULL INSPECTIONS particularly, your judgement about the progress made by pupils with SEN, pupils who speak English as an additional language, and gifted and talented pupils should be summative judgements based on how well pupils are doing in relation to specific targets or goals. You should evaluate the progress made by a representative sample in each case, as appropriate, in accordance with the particular characteristics of the school.

You should ensure that the sample chosen is representative of the types of need found in the school and is also representative of the number supported, as defined by the *Code of Practice on SEN*, including pupils attending a diagnostic unit or resource base. When judging the **achievements of pupils with special educational needs,** find out how the school uses its entry assessment data, test and other assessment data and target setting procedures in individual education plans (IEPs) or in statements to set appropriately challenging targets for groups of SEN pupils. This will help you judge whether the **progress made is good enough.** Obtain different types of evidence, for example progress from records, pupils' responses to questions in class and their performance across the full range of subjects, as well as how well they are learning in small groups and in one-to-one teaching.

All this evidence should help you come to an overall view about the **achievements of pupils with special educational needs,** including the progress towards the targets specifically set in IEPs or annual review. Make sure you record on *Evidence Forms* the gains pupils make in knowledge, skills and understanding, so that you can substantiate and illustrate your judgements, making a distinction here as appropriate between pupils with specific needs.

To judge the achievements of gifted and talented pupils, find out if the school uses its assessment data to identify and make provision for these pupils. In schools which appear to have few high attainers, check from your observations of pupils' work in lessons, and by talking to pupils, whether the results and the school's assessment data accurately reflect pupils' aptitudes.

In schools where **gifted and talented pupils** are identified, be sure you gather sufficient evidence to judge whether their progress is good enough. In schools where gifted and talented pupils are present but not adequately catered for, gather sufficient evidence to substantiate judgements about their underachievement.

Example 2.1.8

Achievement – most able pupils: extract from a report

The school's programme of support for the most able students is highly effective. It is very well organised and is based on very good identification of a pupil's potential for high attainment. The programme has a set of rigorous criteria for identifying the more able, very able and those with particular talents. Each subject department has developed and shared the characteristics of high attainment in that subject. The programme helps to develop common features and a blend of in-class and out-of-school provision, with, for example, occasional talks by local post-graduate students and young executives.

The programme is well implemented in practice and the standards achieved by very able students are unusually high. Samples of work in Y10 English showed fluent, expressive and mature writing with the stamp of originality in vocabulary and structure. Standards of mathematics in an 'early entry' group in Y9 were very high with a speed of mathematics thinking and the ability to hypothesise intelligently and make connections.

[Overall: excellent (1)]

To evaluate the **achievements of pupils for whom English is an additional language,** you should find out their competence in English by reference to the levels in the National Curriculum, because this will determine the kind of help they need. Gather sufficient evidence from lessons where these pupils are receiving support, or from any specialist teaching, so that you can make judgements on their progress. Make sure you record on *Evidence Forms* gains in all aspects of English to substantiate your judgements. For further detail on reading and writing competence see the booklet *English as an Additional Language* published in *Inspecting Subjects and Aspects, 11–18.*

Example 2.1.9

> ### Progress of pupils with English as an additional language
>
> *Drama was used very effectively in Year 10 to extend and deepen pupils' understanding of the current fiction text* Animal Farm. *This focused on the oral exchange of views in a courtroom scene, where Napoleon was put on trial for betraying the principles of the revolution, giving particular scope and opportunity to pupils with English as an additional language. They were given good models of the way in which points are made and questions are used in the convention of the courtroom and were able to consolidate and extend them as they asked questions or responded, as witnesses.*
>
> [Overall: very good (2)]

☐ How well do pupils achieve?

This is an important judgement for which you have a range of evidence.

In the classroom, you will find out:

- what pupils know, what they understand and what they can do, and you should test their understanding and ability to apply their knowledge to related problems;

- how pupils are responding to the educational demands made on them and whether they are challenged enough;

- what work they have done, and to what standard.

Additional evidence should include:

- how the school's results compare with those of similar schools;

- tests, assessments and other records which show progress over time;

- value-added measures if available.

You should also take into account other factors which help decide whether achievements are as high as they could or should be, for example:

- any special educational needs which have been identified;

- whether pupils' education has been disrupted by frequent changes of school;

- whether the fact that English is not the first language poses barriers to progress;

- minority ethnic pupils, particularly refugees and asylum seekers.

Achievements are likely to be high where pupils are working at full stretch, constantly engaged in thinking or doing things which are unfamiliar and which require effort, concentration and perseverance. Achievement is likely to be too low if pupils either fail to understand their work and what is expected, or when they are consistently successful at tasks which they have already mastered. You should consider whether pupils are making as much progress as possible, from the time they join the school, and whether by the time they leave the school they are well equipped for the next stage in education or employment. How well do they apply themselves to their work?

2.2 PUPILS' ATTITUDES, VALUES AND PERSONAL DEVELOPMENT

Inspectors must evaluate and report on pupils':

☐ attitudes to the school;

☐ behaviour, including the incidence of exclusions;

☐ personal development and relationships;

☐ attendance.

In determining their judgements, inspectors should consider the extent to which pupils or students:

• are keen and eager to come to school;

• show interest in school life, and are involved in the range of activities the school provides;

• behave well in lessons and around the school, are courteous, trustworthy and show respect for property;

• form constructive relationships with one another, and with teachers and other adults;

• work in an atmosphere free from oppressive behaviour, including bullying, sexism and racism;

• reflect on what they do and understand its impact on others;

• respect other people's differences, particularly their feelings, values and beliefs;

• show initiative and are willing to take responsibility;

• have high levels of attendance and low levels of unauthorised absence.

INSPECTION FOCUS

This section is concerned with how well pupils and students respond to school in terms of their attitudes to learning, their behaviour, their values and personal development. The criteria cover pupils' responses to what the staff provide, through their teaching and personal example, the curriculum, and the school's provision for spiritual, moral, social and cultural development.

For all pupils and students good behaviour is a pre-requisite for effective learning.

You also need to evaluate pupils' attitudes and their impact on how they learn and the standards they achieve. Attitudes are influenced by what teachers do. You will learn much about the ethos of the school by observing the quality of relationships between pupils from different backgrounds and between pupils and staff.

MAKING JUDGEMENTS

Make full use of the parents' meeting and discussions with pupils to gain their perspectives on what it is like to be a pupil in this school. Most pupils enjoy coming to school; find out what it is about the provision that makes this so.

Use your evaluation of pupils' attitudes in lessons and your contacts with, and observations of, them at other times to decide how good attitudes and behaviour are in this school. You will need to find out the extent to which attitudes and behaviour help or hinder pupils' learning. In making your judgement about the values and personal development of the pupils, take into account your conclusions about how well the school provides opportunities for pupils' spiritual, moral, social and cultural development, and how the school helps pupils develop into responsible individuals, and relate well to each other.

The following characteristics illustrate where to pitch judgements about the attitudes, values and personal development of pupils.

Very good or excellent	Pupils and students are keen to come to school and are quickly and positively involved in a wide range of activities. They make the most of the opportunities provided. They behave very well in and around the school and work constructively and co-operatively in groups and productively on their own. Pupils and students have respect for each other, and show a mature understanding of each other and of different viewpoints. Misbehaviour is very rare, punctuality is good. The attendance figures for the school are above the national average and attendance in Years 10 and 11 is good. Exclusions are very low for this type of school.
Satisfactory or better	Most pupils like, or at least accept, school. They are willing to help each other and their teachers and take part in activities outside lessons. Their behaviour is good most of the time and they are able and can be relied on to work on their own. Pupils are kind and considerate and show respect for each other and a willingness to listen. They are mainly punctual to lessons and rarely absent. Exclusions are low.

However, attitudes, values and personal development **cannot be satisfactory** if there are more than isolated instances of:

- disruptive, aggressive or intimidating behaviour;

- racist attitudes or sexist language or behaviour;

- significant truancy or lack of punctuality;

- marked unruliness in one or more classes.

Example 2.2.1

Extract from an inspection report of a secondary school

Pupils respond very well to the positive climate for learning. They take challenging opportunities very well and demonstrate exceptional maturity and excellent behaviour. All expect to work hard and to concentrate on learning more and improving. Pupils share their views and solutions readily and contribute confidently and supportively in group or class discussions. Pupils are independent and self-reliant and are confident with creative ways of working. Virtually all pupils are courteous, polite and co-operative, and show respect for each other and for teachers and other adults in the school. There is no evidence of aggressive or racist behaviour.

[Contributes to judgements of excellent attitudes (1) and behaviour (1)]

REPORTING REQUIREMENTS

SUMMARY REPORT	In both FULL and SHORT INSPECTIONS complete the table PUPILS' ATTITUDES, VALUES AND PERSONAL DEVELOPMENT. Write brief evaluations on the strengths and weaknesses under the table as supporting text. If any of these feature in the improvement of the school, record this in HOW THE SCHOOL HAS IMPROVED SINCE ITS LAST INSPECTION. Any aspects that are particularly good or need to improve should be reported under WHAT THE SCHOOL DOES WELL or WHAT COULD BE IMPROVED.
SHORT INSPECTIONS	If pupils' attitudes, values or personal development are either a strength or a weakness of the school this should be reported as a section in the commentary.
FULL INSPECTIONS	Report in full under the schedule heading PUPILS' ATTITUDES, VALUES AND PERSONAL DEVELOPMENT.

GUIDANCE ON USING THE CRITERIA

☐ Pupils' attitudes to the school

Are pupils and students keen to come to school? Do they show interest in school life and are they involved in the range of activities the school provides?

Notice how students come into the school at the start of the day. See if they move around the school calmly and with purpose. Are they pleased to show you around and discuss things with you? Students and pupils who are interested and involved will be keen to work in lessons, answer questions, engage with the task in hand, participate in the range of activities provided and show enthusiasm to get as much out of school as possible.

When attitudes to the school are good, consider the reasons why. These may include:

■ good teaching and interesting lessons;

■ pupils being clear about the way they should behave;

■ successful links between home and school;

■ the school values the cultural traditions, aspirations and values pupils bring with them from home and their communities.

Consider the attitudes of different groups of pupils to the school and, where there are differences, find out why. See if the school is aware of them and find out what is being done, if anything, about them.

Example 2.2.2

Extract from a full inspection report

There is a wide participation in the range of lunchtime activities (chess club, school choir, archaeology club) and the range of after-school activities (drama, athletics, rounders, astronomy, art, homework club) which covers boys and girls equally although mainly from Key Stage 3. The group of children from Somalian refugee families who have recently joined the local community have been slow to become involved with the full range of school activities. The school has established a regular meeting with parents from this group, and provided support for learning English for parents through the Modern Foreign Languages department. As a result, Somalian parents and children, together with the drama and dance staff and children in the school, are preparing a drama documentary called 'Somalian Sunrise', for the school summer arts festival.

[Reflects very good attitudes (2), excellent extra-curricular provision (1)]

☐ Behaviour, including the incidence of exclusions

Do pupils and students behave well in lessons and around the school, are they courteous, trustworthy and respectful of the property of others?

Evaluate behaviour throughout the school day, in classrooms and at break and lunchtime. Notice if pupils are polite to each other and to adults, and if they look after their own property as well as that of others. Look at the behaviour policy in the school, and find out if pupils contributed to it or know about it. Take account of the views expressed by parents either at the parents' meeting and/or in the questionnaires. In a good school teachers and support staff will have to spend little time seeking to establish order and discipline.

You must evaluate the reasons for any exclusions from the school, both permanent and fixed term. The *PICSI report* gives comparative data. Establish whether the school's procedures are correct and whether exclusions are monitored with respect to gender, ethnicity and pupils' ability. Ask what the school does with this information and the impact that it has on policy and practice. Consider the number of exclusions, the number of pupils involved, the reasons for the exclusions and the length of time out. You should consider how well the school re-integrates pupils after a period of exclusion. Whether or not the school is designated an In-School Centre by the DfEE you must evaluate its success at keeping pupils working who are at risk from exclusion.

Example 2.2.3

Record of Corporate Judgements: *behaviour weaknesses*

- *Difficult and troublesome responses to teachers in English and science Y8. A significant minority of pupils challenge nature of work set, being dismissive and inattentive. Poor standards of behaviour; much incidental chat, turning into rudeness when checked.*

- *Unpleasant personal remarks by three boys about girls unchecked in history Y9. Shouting across the class, personal vendettas from break-time continued.*

- *Insolence to teacher on duty in corridor at break by group of Y10 boys. Doors banged, litter dropped. Teacher took no action – felt unsupported.*

- *Pupils in Y9 find it difficult to work alone, very poor behaviour in library when engaged in research task; misuse of CD-ROM and of information files. Rude to parent volunteer helper.*

[Contributes to a judgement of poor behaviour (6)]

☐ Personal development and relationships

Do pupils and students show initiative and are they willing to take responsibility?

Find out if, for example, pupils and students in the sixth form:

- take an active part in the day-to-day life and organisation of the school;

- show by their attitudes that they see themselves as part of the school community;

- support each other;

- are able to plan and organise their own work and study without supervision;

- cope confidently with the pressures and opportunities of school life.

Do pupils form constructive relationships with one another, and with teachers and other adults?

Most of the evidence about relationships and personal development will come from your observations of pupils around the school. Look for evidence of pupils working and playing well together, particularly those from different minority ethnic backgrounds. Check if those with special educational needs are also included. Evaluate how well the pupils have learned to respect differences and understand the feelings, values and beliefs of others.

Do pupils reflect on and understand the impact of what they do on others? Do they respect the feelings, values and beliefs of others?

Look to see how far pupils are able to listen to what others have to say and respond positively to ideas, views and feelings different from their own. Evaluate:

- how good pupils are at reflecting on and discussing their own behaviour, feelings and experience;

- how far pupils see things for what they are, listen to what others have to say and are interested in and tolerant of ideas, views and feelings different from their own;

41

- how far pupils recognise, understand and respect different values and beliefs, attitudes, and social and cultural traditions;

- how far pupils reflect on and understand the impact of what they do on others;

- how far they engage in discussion and are prepared to change their minds as a result of reasoned debate.

Example 2.2.4

Extract from a lesson observation

In a Year 10 history lesson, with very careful coverage of the difficult moral and philosophical issues arising from the Holocaust, European history 1940–1945 and the issues of collaboration, the teacher leads pupils to a wider awareness of historical events, and to make links with current European and African ethnic conflict. Pupils discuss private and public actions and beliefs – 'Should you do what you are told?' – 'When does armed resistance to evil become an obligation, if at all?' They show considerable insight and some courage in this debate. The teacher reads an extract from Rose Blanche, *a picture book, to focus on action, values and beliefs at the end of the lesson and to illustrate the central points of the debate.*

[Contributes to an excellent lesson (1) with pupils demonstrating very good reflection and understanding (2)]

Do pupils work in an atmosphere free from oppressive behaviour, such as bullying, sexism and racism?

Pupils can occasionally feel bullied or intimidated. Talk to pupils to find out if they know who to go to if they have a problem, how it is dealt with and whether they feel supported.

You need to assess how aware the adults in the school are and what steps they take to promote positive role models and counter negative attitudes throughout the school. Evaluate the extent to which pupils are encouraged to work in mixed ethnic and gender groups. If there is evidence of racism, find out what the school is doing to combat this.

Example 2.2.5

Extract from an inspection report

All adults in the school, from teachers to site management and cleaning staff, have had training to ensure that the school's wide range of ethnic groups becomes a source of strength and an impetus to high achievement. There is a clear and consistent sense of purpose in all adult–pupil contact, which promotes confidence and gives a human dimension to the school. The school's work in this area has been accompanied by a steady improvement in examination performance over the last two years. The excellent ethos is likely to have contributed to this improvement.

☐ Attendance

Are there high levels of attendance?

Use the data in the *PICSI report* to relate a school's attendance to the national picture. You need only make further inquiries if it is below 92 per cent for the school or 90 per cent *in any year group* or if you have concerns, for example about a downward trend. In this case, check how parents are supported in ensuring the regular attendance of their child and if there are straightforward procedures for reporting absence. Check that registers are completed each morning and afternoon, and that they conform to the latest guidance. Look at the strategies the school uses in partnership with the Education Welfare Service to reduce the levels of unauthorised absence.

The school's own analysis of attendance, in relation to all schools, in its application of the principle of 'comparison' within the best value framework, is a useful source of information. You should consider the school's own analysis of attendance data, especially if there are, for example, differences between year or ethnic groups.

3. HOW WELL ARE PUPILS OR STUDENTS TAUGHT?

Inspectors must evaluate and report on:

☐ the quality of teaching, judged in terms of its impact on learning and what makes it successful or not.

Inspectors must include evaluations of:

• **how well the skills of literacy and numeracy are taught,** particularly to any pupils of secondary age whose reading, writing or numeracy is poor;

• **how well the teaching meets the needs of all its pupils and students,** taking account of their age, gender, ethnicity, capability, special educational needs, whether they are gifted and talented, and the needs of those for whom English is an additional language;

• **the teaching in each subject, commenting on any variations between subjects and year groups;**

☐ how well pupils and students learn and make progress.

In determining their judgements, inspectors should consider the extent to which teachers:

• show good subject knowledge and understanding in the way they present and discuss their subject;

• are technically competent in teaching basic skills;

• plan effectively, setting clear objectives that pupils understand;

• challenge and inspire pupils, expecting the most of them, so as to deepen their knowledge and understanding;

• use methods which enable all pupils to learn effectively;

• manage pupils well and insist on high standards of behaviour;

• use time, support staff and other resources, especially information and communications technology, effectively;

• assess pupils' work thoroughly and use assessments to help and encourage pupils to overcome difficulties;

• use homework effectively to reinforce and/or extend what is learned in school;

and the extent to which pupils and students:

• acquire new knowledge or skills, develop ideas and increase their understanding;

• apply intellectual, physical or creative effort in their work;

• are productive and work at a good pace;

• show interest in their work, are able to sustain concentration and think and learn for themselves;

• understand what they are doing, how well they have done and how they can improve.

INSPECTION FOCUS

Evaluation of the quality and impact of teaching is central to inspection. Teaching is fundamental to the quality of education provided by the school and the main avenue through which the school contributes to pupils' attainment, progress and attitudes. The effectiveness of teaching and the consequent rate, breadth, depth and consolidation of pupils' learning are intrinsically connected. It is the skill of rigorous and perceptive inspection to find, illustrate and evaluate the links between the two.

When evaluating the quality of teaching and learning in the school, the process of education, you should concentrate on these priorities:

- evaluating the quality of teaching, in terms of how effective it is;

- identifying which aspects of teaching work best, or least well;

- recording and reporting these insights so as to illustrate good practice and to explain weaknesses clearly so as to provide a basis for improvement.

In every lesson observed, you should consider:

- the subject matter, its context and relevance, and how it relates to the pupils and what they have done before;

- the methods used and structure of the lesson, evaluating each of the lesson's components where these are distinct;

- the pupils, what they are required to do and how they do it, noticing the extent to which the lesson is engaging or addressing the needs of all of them as fully as it should.

TEACHING

Your insight stems from the detailed classroom observation of teaching and pupils at work, complemented by the depth of understanding pupils show in discussion with you and your analysis of the quality and standards of the work they have done. This will enable you to see whether pupils are learning as much, as quickly and as well as you expect, and to judge the quality of the teaching.

You need to explain your judgements by exemplifying what it is the teacher actually does that helps to make learning successful or not, and you need to know what could be done to improve it further. Do not become side-tracked in the pursuit of individual criteria at the expense of missing the key points in a lesson. You should give particular attention to how well the skills of literacy and numeracy are taught and how well the needs of all pupils are met.

Judging teaching in subjects

In SHORT INSPECTIONS, you judge the quality of teaching overall based on the lessons seen, across subjects. However, much of your evidence will stem from seeking to verify the hypotheses established in the pre-inspection commentary, with a focus on English, mathematics and science.

On FULL INSPECTIONS, judgements about teaching in subjects are abstracted from *Evidence Forms* and recorded in the *Inspection Notebook*. Use the separate guidance on the inspection of subjects in *Inspecting Subjects 11–18* to identify the overall quality and strengths and weaknesses in teaching in every lesson observed.

Judging the overall quality of teaching in the school

Teaching overall is likely to be unsatisfactory if more than approximately one in ten lessons are so judged. If these contain poor or very poor teaching, or the proportion is higher than one in eight, you will need to consider whether the school has serious weaknesses. Once the proportion of unsatisfactory teaching reaches one lesson in five it is very likely to be in need of special measures. If most of the teaching in the school is good, with much of it very good or better, and no unsatisfactory teaching, the overall quality of teaching could be judged very good.

Reporting on teaching in the school needs to be crystal clear in terms of what works, what does not, why and what should be done about it. Make sure your messages on how well pupils are taught are consistent with the other two major areas of inspection: standards, and the leadership and management of the school. Excellent leadership and management, for example, do not sit comfortably with teaching which is simply satisfactory with a few good lessons.

Example 3.1

Record of Corporate Judgements: *strengths and weaknesses in teaching*

Strengths:

- *Good subject knowledge, with material matched to range of need and attainment, particularly in KS3 in MFL, MA, art [EFs 2, 3, 10, 14, 16, 23, 51, 72, 75, 76, 111]*

- *Clarity of the learning and progress expected during the lesson and made clear to pupils in science in Year 10, maths Years 10, 11, and in music Years 7– 9 [EFs 8, 13, 20, 64, 65, 98]*

- *Effective use of whole class teaching in Y10 drama and Y9 history. Good, well-organised group work in science with lower ability sets in Y8 and in French in Y10 – maximum opportunities for spoken language [EFs 18, 32, 33, 39, 44, 86,89, 103]*

- *High standards of challenge to thinking, and good responses in sixth form work in history, geography and science [EFs 28, 42, 63, 115]*

- *Good homework to consolidate and extend learning throughout KS4 – particularly design and technology and science [Many references, EFs 35, 40, 59, 98]*

Weaknesses:

- *Poor levels of learning in RE , in KS3 – poor explanation and questioning, poor pace of work*

- *Lack of clear purpose, with pupils drifting, with little sense of direction in their reading of class fiction in English in Y7. Pupils underachieve in reading*

- *Poor behaviour and poor progress in history in Y8, with insufficient attention to sequence of events and to the use and understanding of sources*

Overall evaluation:

Good teaching in KS4 and sixth form. Lack of planning and rigour in some KS3 lessons. Maths and science stronger than English in core subjects in both Key Stages. Reading in English a key area for improvement in the intake year.

[Contributes to a judgement of good teaching (3)]

Judging the quality of teaching in lessons

The following characteristics illustrate where to pitch judgements about how well pupils are taught in lessons.

Very good or excellent	The teaching of skills and subject matter is knowledgeable, stimulating and exciting; it uses imaginative resources and makes intellectual and creative demands on pupils to take their learning further. Challenging questions are used to consolidate, extend and verify what pupils know and understand. The methods chosen are well geared to the particular focus and demands of the lesson and make the most productive use of the time available. Relationships in the classroom provide a confident and positive atmosphere in which achievement flourishes. Pupils are keen to learn, rise to challenges in creative ways and think further. They work well for extended periods of time and as a result gains in knowledge and understanding are very high.
Satisfactory or better	The teaching of basic skills and subject content is clear and accurate, using explanation and demonstration and involving all pupils. The organisation of the lesson allows most pupils to keep up with the work and to complete tasks in the time available. Teachers check pupils' understanding and ensure they remain on task. The relationship between the pupils and teacher is such that pupils can get on with their work and know how well they have done. Most pupils show sound application to their work.

However teaching **cannot be satisfactory** if any one of the following is present:

- teachers' knowledge of subjects is not good enough to promote demanding work;
- basic skills are not taught effectively;
- a significant minority of pupils are not engaged in the lesson;
- lessons are poorly planned and organised and time is wasted;
- there are weaknesses in controlling the class;
- pupils do not know what they are doing;
- pupils are not making progress.

Example 3.2

Extract from a subject report: teaching of English – Julius Caesar

Pupils learned little in the lesson about the nature of Shakespearean language and its verbal and emotional structure. They made no progress in their understanding because of a line-by-line translation of Mark Anthony's speech into modern English by the teacher, whose own knowledge of blank verse and patterns of dramatic rhetoric did not match the demands and complexity of the text. Because the material was never given a dramatic context, pupils' understanding both of the speaker and the situation remained at an unsatisfactory level. No demands made on pupils' imagination and no opportunities for critical and interpretative reading. Behaviour was dutifully acquiescent.

[Overall: poor teaching (6)]

REPORTING REQUIREMENTS

SUMMARY REPORT

In both FULL and SHORT INSPECTIONS you must complete the table TEACHING AND LEARNING. In FULL INSPECTIONS, and where possible in SHORT INSPECTIONS, write brief comments about the quality of teaching in English and mathematics; strengths and weaknesses in teaching; how well the school meets the needs of all pupils; the percentages of satisfactory or better, very good or better and unsatisfactory or worse teaching; and particular strengths and weaknesses in pupils' learning.

If any of these are a feature in improvement in the school, report this in the section HOW THE SCHOOL HAS IMPROVED SINCE ITS LAST INSPECTION.

If any aspects of teaching are particularly good or need to improve you must report these under WHAT THE SCHOOL DOES WELL or WHAT COULD BE IMPROVED in the commentary. Complete the data tables in Part C of the report including the data on teaching.

SHORT INSPECTIONS

In the commentary, expand your judgements on teaching as reported in either WHAT THE SCHOOL DOES WELL or WHAT COULD BE IMPROVED. Complete the data tables in Part C of the report including the data on teaching.

FULL INSPECTIONS

Report fully under the heading HOW WELL ARE PUPILS TAUGHT? Complete the data tables in Part C of the report, including the data on teaching.

GUIDANCE ON USING THE CRITERIA

In order to stress the importance of evaluating teaching through its impact, this guidance puts learning first. The criteria for learning are encapsulated by the questions: to what extent are the pupils engaged? challenged? extended? For teaching, the questions include: are pupils taught the right things in an effective manner and at the right pace?

☐ How well pupils learn and make progress

Do pupils acquire new knowledge or skills, develop ideas and increase their understanding?

In forming your judgements about the acquisition of knowledge, skills or understanding, take every opportunity to relate this to the work done previously. Learning may be consolidated or may cover new ground in the lesson you observe. Your judgements should, where possible, be referenced to what has gone before. The learning objectives identified by the teacher will help you to ask pupils relevant questions and to judge whether the teaching and learning are well matched to the pupils' age and attainment. Whenever you can, record specific examples of how the teaching helps the pupils to understand more.

Examination of work and discussion with pupils will also help you to decide if the work in hand builds on pupils' current knowledge, understanding or skills, in order that the pupils can make progress. When you analyse samples of work, focus on evidence of progress over time, within year groups. Look for consistency of approach and content between classes covering the same age range, where relevant. The completed *Evidence Forms* on the scrutiny of pupils' work should provide detailed information about the rate, quantity and quality of pupils' learning, not simply a list of the content covered year by year.

Discussion with pupils about what they are doing can give you an insight into how they acquire new knowledge and skills, and increase their understanding across the subjects of the curriculum. On SHORT INSPECTIONS, this may be your prime source of evidence of work in some subjects.

Do pupils apply intellectual, physical or creative effort in their work and are they working productively and at a good pace?

Most pupils will make an effort in their work if the teaching makes demands and provides the encouragement which enables them to do so. You need to judge, therefore, the extent to which pupils are engaged in their work, whether the effort involved is enough or too much, and whether it is worthwhile in relation to what is learnt. Every lesson should contribute in some way towards the pupils' development or consolidation of knowledge, skills or understanding. The pupils should be able to explain what they have done and what they have learnt at the end of each lesson. Pupils are far more likely to apply effort in their work when they see why they are working in a particular way, and why what they are required to understand is important.

The amount of work pupils do, the extent to which they have to concentrate and their attitude to the tasks, will indicate if they are working to capacity. Pupils do not always work at a good pace unless the teacher expects them to. During lesson observations, try to return to the same pupils more than once to judge if they are working well enough and getting through the required amount. This also provides evidence about the teacher's use of time. Check to see if lessons start on time and if they finish crisply with a succinct review of the learning rather than peter out or over-run. Good teaching routines encourage pupils to manage their own time well and to get through what is required in the time available.

Do pupils show interest in their work? Are they able to sustain concentration and thinking and learn for themselves? Do pupils understand what they are doing, how well they have done and how they can improve?

Pupils are likely to show interest and understanding when the tasks, activities and challenges presented are lively and interesting. Good teachers constantly relate new learning to old, encouraging pupils to make the links between subjects and to think imaginatively for themselves.

Successful teachers make clear to the pupils what they are expected to learn, the standards that are expected, and how they can do even better next time.

To summarise, you can expect learning to be effective when the teaching is good. The pupils will be keen and interested from the beginning of the lesson. They are clear about what they are doing and why they are doing it. They can see the links with their earlier learning and have some ideas about how it then could be developed further. The pupils want to know more and take responsibility for finding out more of their own accord. They understand what is good about their work and how it can be improved. They support one another and know when and where to go for help.

☐ **The quality of teaching, judged in terms of its impact on pupils' learning and what makes it successful or not**

Do teachers show good subject knowledge and understanding in the way they present and discuss their subject?

Evaluate the success of teaching and what makes it so. You can judge teachers' subject knowledge by observing, for example:

■ how competently they teach the content of the National Curriculum programmes of study, and the RE syllabus; the requirements for public examinations and programmes of vocational study;

■ how competently they plan the learning in the subject or area of work, showing a good understanding of the way the subject develops;

■ their skills in asking subject specific questions which help pupils to understand and which extend their thinking;

■ how well they explain new ideas in a way that make sense to pupils;

■ how well they draw on their knowledge of how pupils learn when presenting them with new experiences or information;

■ how well they use equipment, artefacts and resources to interest and challenge the pupils;

■ their ability to deepen the thinking in the subject for all pupils and stretch the more able.

Where pupils in the secondary stage require teaching in the skills of literacy and numeracy, refer to the guidance in the *Handbook for Inspecting Primary and Nursery Schools*, Teaching section. You must evaluate any use of the National Literacy Strategy, for example in Year 7.

Example 3.3

> ### A bland report on patchy mathematics teaching in a 9–13 middle school
>
> *Teaching in mathematics is just satisfactory overall. In nearly half the lessons observed it was good or better. It was distinctly better in Key Stage 2 than Key Stage 3, with the best teaching observed in Year 5 and the top sets. Most teachers use short mental mathematics sessions to good effect at the beginning of lessons, particularly with younger pupils, getting lessons off to a good brisk start, using strategies that involve all pupils. In Year 7 an investigative approach as to whether changing the order of two operations, for example addition and multiplication, affects the answer, gave pupils the opportunity to gain real understanding of inverse operations rather than rote learning of rules. There is good use of practical resources, such as pin-boards, to explore conservation of area and finding the area of irregular shapes. In spite of only two of the twelve teachers taking mathematics having a mathematics qualification, subject expertise was sound or better in nearly all lessons, the exception being in a Year 8 class, where pupils were coasting. The few other instances of teaching which was unsatisfactory occurred where teachers had not taken a mathematics class in previous years. Work in pupils' books is marked, but not graded. Written comments to help pupils improve are inconsistent, ranging from explaining mistakes to the unhelpful 'you can do better'. Worthwhile homework is regularly set according to the school timetable.*
>
> [Overall: satisfactory teaching (4)]

Do teachers plan effectively, setting clear objectives that pupils understand?

In a lesson, session or sequence of lessons, look for clear objectives for what pupils are to learn, and how these objectives will be achieved. Does planning take into account the differing needs of pupils, such as those with specific difficulties? Whatever form the planning takes, look for evidence of what teachers intend and how they will know if their intentions are met. Once you know what the lesson aims to do, you can ask relevant questions when you talk to the pupils and make accurate judgements about the success or otherwise of the lesson.

If there is time, you should also discuss with teachers how the lesson fits into the longer-term plans and why, for example, they use particular methods. Such discussions provide insight into teachers' planning and their response to changing situations which are not always recorded on paper.

Consider how support staff, if there are any, are involved in planning the teaching and are briefed about what they are expected to do.

Do teachers challenge and inspire pupils, expecting the most of them, so as to deepen their knowledge and understanding?

You may see lessons where teachers advance learning in an atmosphere of imaginative speculation and curiosity, unconstrained by subject boundaries. They provide pointers to new connections and deeper understanding, provoking determined and unexpected contributions from pupils. The challenge lies in the intellectual and imaginative effort needed; the inspiration in the new directions the pupils take. Few teachers can manage this all the time but you should be quick to recognise it and praise it when you see it.

Example 3.4

Extract from a report: English teaching in a school with a sixth form

The quality of teaching is very good; several excellent lessons were seen. Sixth form teaching is of a particularly high academic standard. Teachers know their subject well, and plan and prepare thoroughly. They have high expectations of attainment and behaviour. They are particularly skilled in preparing pupils thoroughly for examinations and this contributes to well-above-average results. Work set is matched skilfully to pupils' levels of attainment. For example, special needs pupils in Year 7 wrote imaginative and lively poems about apples in response to sensitive and well-managed teaching, which enabled pupils to experience their subject through their five senses. The good quality of their work was a direct result of their keen interest, generated by stimulating and well-judged teaching. The pace of teaching is good in most lessons.

In the sixth form, pupils are intellectually stretched through rigorous questioning and insistence on opinions being supported through references to the text. Pupils' work is marked conscientiously and constructively with helpful comments and target-setting. The quality of day-to-day assessment and recording of attainment is very good. Monitoring of pupils' progress is very thorough. The ethos of the department matches closely that of the school.

[Overall: very good teaching (2) with patches of excellence (1)]

Do teachers use methods which enable all pupils to learn effectively?

Consider how well teachers match the methods they use to the purpose of the lesson. The key to the judgements you make is whether these methods and their organisation are likely to result in high standards of work and behaviour for all pupils. If there are any pupils, or groups of pupils, who are not involved and not learning effectively, then you must identify the reasons. Consider specifically whether the methods used support pupils of high attainment, those with special educational needs, and, where relevant, pupils for whom English is an additional language.

You will need to evaluate whether:

- exposition or explanation by the teacher is lively, informative and well structured;
- the teacher's use and style of questions probes pupils' knowledge and understanding, challenges their thinking and engages all pupils;
- practical activity is purposeful and not stereotyped in that pupils are encouraged to think about what they are doing, what they have learned from it and how to improve their work;
- investigations and problem-solving activities help pupils to apply and extend their learning in new contexts;
- the choice of pupil grouping, for example pupils working alone, in pairs or small groups or all together, achieves the objectives for teaching and learning;
- the form of organisation allows the teacher to work efficiently with as many pupils as possible;
- the use of resources stimulates learning and sensitively reflects different groups, cultures and backgrounds;
- the teacher encourages the development of the pupils' imaginative spark and creative and intellectual curiosity;
- the sixth form teaching provides a bridge between the structured learning of Key Stage 4 and the scholarship and the study skills required of advanced work.

The choice of teaching methods is a matter for the school. You must judge whether what is done is effective.

Do teachers manage pupils well and insist on high standards of behaviour?

You should consider the quality of relationships in the classroom and the extent to which teachers create a purposeful working atmosphere.

Some important features, which reduce the incidence of inappropriate behaviour, include the extent to which:

- the teacher exercises authority clearly and fairly from the outset;
- the teacher holds the pupils' attention and involves them in the work in hand, encouraging their concentration and completion of the task;
- the organisation of the work to be done and the grouping of pupils to do it is carried out clearly and efficiently;
- the teacher supports and controls the pupils, intervening according to the needs of individuals and groups;
- there is mutual respect between teacher and pupils and proper habits of work are established and developed;
- the teacher stresses the importance of self-discipline and has expectations of mature behaviour.

Do teachers use time, support staff and other resources, especially information and communications technology (ICT), effectively?

Management of the pupils, time, resources and support promotes good behaviour and effective learning. Resources should be sufficient in quantity and quality, and fitted to the intended work.

Central to your judgements relating to these criteria is the extent to which teachers manage time and resources so that pupils work productively. In effective lessons the pace is usually brisk, but there are occasions when time is needed for reflection and consolidation.

Evaluate whether time is used efficiently and whether pupils know what they have to do and how long they have in which to do it.

As you evaluate the work of teachers in teaching IT capability, check to see that it centres upon the teacher's expectation of pupils in their use of resources and their development or consolidation of knowledge. You need to observe the pupils and the teacher's interaction with them to find out if there is a clearly understood expectation of what the pupils should be doing and why. The activity may be planned to develop IT capability, support learning within the subject or both. How effectively teachers use ICT tools is dependent upon the clarity of their intention and the quality of intervention and support given during the use of ICT. You need to judge whether the intervention by the teacher merely solves technical problems or maintains pupils' attention upon the task. Does it enhance pupils' understanding of IT, the subject or both? When parents or support staff are directed by the teacher to help pupils using ICT, they too need to be aware of what the teacher expects from the use of the ICT and what they should do to ensure the intended learning takes place.

Do teachers assess pupils' work thoroughly and use assessments to help and encourage pupils to overcome difficulties?

Your judgements about teachers' assessment of their pupils should focus on how well teachers look for gains in learning, gaps in knowledge and areas of misunderstanding, through their day to day work with pupils. This will include marking, questioning of individuals and plenary sessions. Clues to the effectiveness of formative assessment are how well the teachers listen and respond to pupils, encourage, and, where appropriate praise them, recognise and handle misconceptions, build on their responses and steer them towards clearer understanding.

Effective teachers encourage pupils to judge the success of their own work and set targets for improvement. They will take full account of the targets set out in individual education plans for pupils with special educational needs.

Do teachers use homework effectively to reinforce and/or extend what is learned in school?

Within the context of the school's policy for homework, you should establish whether homework:

■ is planned to integrate with classwork;

■ is tailored to individual learning needs;

■ helps pupils to learn independently;

■ is regularly and constructively marked.

You should also establish whether parents support and ratify the homework that is done, for example by signing off homework diaries.

How well does the teaching meet the needs of all pupils?

In this *Handbook* references have been made to the importance of evaluating the effectiveness of teaching and learning for all pupils. As an inspector, your thinking about the needs of all pupils and ensuring equal opportunities is not an optional extra but an integral aspect of all the judgements you make about teaching and every other aspect of the work of the school.

In coming to judgements about how well teachers promote and provide for equal opportunities, you will need to assess if the teaching methods, the access to resources and the time of day or year disadvantage any groups of pupils. You will also need to take account of pupils' ages, gender, ethnicity and capability on reaching your conclusions. For example, the choice of texts in English might favour girls; pupils may be regularly withdrawn from mathematics in order to practise reading skills or for instrumental music tuition; the religious background of the pupils prevents them from taking part in activities which promote their spiritual or cultural development; or, unavoidable lateness to school may result in a pupil always missing the introduction to work in science.

You will need to pay particular attention to the school's provision for three identified groups of pupils: those with special educational needs; those who have English as an additional language; and gifted and talented pupils.

How well does the school meet the needs of pupils with special educational needs (SEN)?

When judging how well the teaching meets the needs of pupils with special education needs, look for its impact on the learning of pupils on the register of special educational needs. The effectiveness of planning is important because it enables the special educational needs co-ordinator, or LEA special educational needs support staff, to liaise successfully with subject teachers at different stages, whether the pupils are supported in class or are withdrawn from lessons. Check to see that individual education plans (IEPs) contain clear targets and are sufficiently practical for teachers to implement when support staff are not present.

You will also need to judge the effectiveness of any learning support assistants in providing the right blend of help and challenge, so that pupils do not become too dependent. Record your observations on the gains pupils make towards the targets set and, whenever possible, exemplify the progress made by pupils with particular disabilities when there is a resource base or unit for pupils with special educational needs. Make sure your judgements are consistent with what you are saying about the progress pupils make in HOW HIGH ARE STANDARDS?, and with what you report in the summary.

Example 3.5

Extract from an inspection report: special educational needs

Support for younger pupils with special educational needs is good when small groups, with below-average reading and writing skills, are withdrawn from lessons for additional support. This work is effective. It is complemented by support within classrooms by class teaching assistants. In one literacy lesson, for example, they and parent volunteers worked with small groups to support reading. However, such help is not often used effectively. The assistants can spend much of the lesson sitting passively by the targeted pupil while the teacher is talking, opportunities for small group working with an adult being missed. Targets in individual education plans are not yet fully reflected in lesson planning for pupils' individual needs. Where they are, such as in physical education, pupils make better progress.

[Withdrawal support good (3), in-class support poor (6). Overall: unsatisfactory (5)]

How well does the school meet the needs of pupils with English as an additional language?

You will need to evaluate whether the planning and teaching methods take account of the language and learning needs of pupils with English as an additional language (EAL). This involves the identification of those who need additional support; not just when they are in the early stages of learning English, but also those at more advanced levels whose literacy skills often fail to do justice to their academic potential. Giving appropriate support will consist of some or all of the following:

- ensuring pupils have opportunities for supported speaking and listening;
- providing effective models of spoken and written language (for example, through 'writing frames');
- understanding how the first language can be used to support the learning of others;
- using high-quality, culturally relevant visual aids and other resources;
- providing bilingual support assistants.

In inspecting EAL, you should look to see whether all the work is firmly placed within the National Curriculum. Withdrawal of pupils from lessons should be kept to a minimum, and their teaching needs to contain the same features as those outlined above.

How well does the school meet the needs of gifted and talented pupils?

To reach their full potential, gifted and talented pupils need challenging tasks that stretch them intellectually. You need to explore:

- how the school identifies its gifted and talented pupils;

- the awareness of teachers of the needs of these pupils;

- the willingness of teachers to adapt and adjust to take account of pupils' rapid development;

- the school's strategies for ensuring that all teachers are able to share in providing the level of subject support needed;

- how the school draws on sources of support for gifted and talented pupils.

4. HOW GOOD ARE THE CURRICULAR AND OTHER OPPORTUNITIES OFFERED TO PUPILS OR STUDENTS?

Inspectors must evaluate and report on:

☐ the quality and range of opportunities for learning provided by the school for all pupils, highlighting features which are particular strengths and weaknesses in the foundation subjects, Key Stages and post-16;

including specific comment on:

- **extra-curricular activities** including study support;

- **the provision made for personal, social and health education,** including sex education and attention to drug misuse;

- **work related education,** including careers education and guidance for secondary age pupils;

- **the quality of links with the community and with other schools, colleges or initial teacher training consortia;**

☐ whether the school meets statutory curriculum requirements, including provision of religious education where appropriate;

☐ how well the school cultivates pupils' personal – including spiritual, moral, social and cultural – development.

In determining their judgements, inspectors should consider the extent to which the school:

- provides a broad range of worthwhile opportunities which meet the interests, aptitudes and particular needs of pupils, including those having special educational needs;

- has effective strategies for teaching the basic skills of literacy and numeracy;

- provides enrichment through its extra-curricular provision including support for learning outside the school day;

- is socially inclusive by ensuring equality of access and opportunity for all pupils;

- provides pupils with the knowledge and insights into values and beliefs and enables them to reflect on their experiences in a way which develops their spiritual awareness and self-knowledge;

- promotes principles which distinguish right from wrong;

- encourages pupils to take responsibility, show initiative and develop an understanding of living in a community;

- teaches pupils to appreciate their own cultural traditions and the diversity and richness of other cultures;

- provides effectively for personal and social education, including health education, sex education and attention to drug misuse;

- has links with the community which contribute to pupils' learning;

- has constructive relationships with partner institutions such as link schools and colleges.

INSPECTION FOCUS

You should evaluate the extent to which the content and organisation of the curriculum provide access to the full range of learning experiences and promote the high achievement and personal development of all pupils. The curriculum comprises all the planned activities within and beyond the timetabled day.

The school should meet all it is required to by statute in Key Stage 2 in middle-deemed secondary schools, Key Stages 3 and 4, and syllabus requirements at GCSE and post-16 courses.

You will need to refer to the appropriate section in *Form S3*, the school self-audit, to gauge the school's perception of how far it meets statutory curriculum requirements. Your analysis of the information from these sources should enable you to raise pertinent questions with the school and to focus on areas which may need to be followed up during the inspection. If everything is in order and the school has made its provision on the basis of what is right for its pupils, then do not waste time looking further. You should only pursue further evidence if you suspect there is a significant problem in terms of what the pupils are entitled to receive, or if there is an area or subject of the curriculum that is particularly good.

Effective schools help pupils to become confident people with enduring values, able to contribute effectively in society. The experiences offered are rich and stimulating, contributing to the personal development of all individuals and so helping them prepare for life as adults.

In your assessment of the curriculum offered to pupils you should find out what the school is really good at. Take note of any areas of excellence. The good school will ensure that the curriculum covers all the key aspects of personal development, providing especially for **spiritual, moral, social and cultural development,** meets the needs of all pupils and responds appropriately to current Qualifications and Curriculum Authority (QCA) Guidance.

Within the framework of '**best value**' (*see Annex 1*), the principle of 'challenge' means that the school should know why its curriculum has been planned as it has. Part of your work is to explore this; in particular, how the school has arrived at the balance of the statutory to the non-statutory curriculum and how the school checks that it is providing what parents want when, for example deciding to offer a particular course.

The evidence you gather will be common to all inspections; however, in SHORT INSPECTIONS you are only required to make judgements and report on the three sections that relate to the quality and range of the curriculum, to the statutory requirements, and to pupils' personal development.

MAKING JUDGEMENTS

A wide variety of evidence contributes to the evaluation of the curriculum. Before the inspection refer to *Form S2* and *S3* to gauge the school's perception of how far it meets the statutory curriculum requirements and the DfEE recommendations for 'taught time' for each Key Stage each week. If the taught time falls below the recommended minimum, you must report it. Form an impression of the quality of what the school offers through your reading of the prospectus and other documents. This impression will be reinforced or rejected once you begin gathering evidence in the school.

The following characteristics illustrate where to pitch judgements about the quality of the curriculum.

Very good or excellent	The curriculum interprets statutory requirements including the required elements within the National Curriculum subjects in a stimulating way, encouraging high achievement, and provides for religious education in accordance with an agreed syllabus. Depending on the needs of students, there is also work-related provision of high quality. It uses resources from within and outside the school very effectively to enrich the curriculum. High priority is given to pupils' personal development through opportunities for pupils to take responsibility and initiative and become aware of their part in the school and wider community. Pupils debate and reflect on moral and social issues, appreciate what is right and wrong, and respect the differences and similarities between people, their values and beliefs, drawing on pupils' own cultural, religious and family beliefs.
Satisfactory or better	The curriculum meets the statutory requirements and offers work-related courses as appropriate. Reasonable use is made of resources within the community; visits and other activities are planned to contribute to pupils' learning. Some opportunities for responsibility and initiative are provided. Most pupils understand the differences between right and wrong, and respect the traditions, values and beliefs of others.

However, the curriculum **cannot be satisfactory** if:

- statutory requirements, including any significant aspects of the core subjects, are not met, and/or;

- opportunities for promoting essential skills are neglected;

- it does little to inculcate respect, tolerance and good behaviour;

- it is unduly narrow in opportunities for personal development, curricular enrichment or work-related learning.

In SHORT INSPECTIONS, extensive evaluation of curricular provision is neither possible nor desirable, but must include whether or not it meets statutory requirements and how well it provides for the spiritual, moral, social and cultural development of pupils.

Where the school has a sixth form, the report should evaluate the quality, range and cost-effectiveness of the post-16 curriculum, including the use made of link courses or other partnership arrangements.

REPORTING REQUIREMENTS

SUMMARY REPORT	In all inspections, the first boxes of the table headed OTHER ASPECTS OF THE SCHOOL must be completed, with comment on particular strengths and weaknesses, and any areas that do not meet statutory requirements.
	If any of these are a feature of improvement in the school they should be recorded in the section HOW THE SCHOOL HAS IMPROVED SINCE ITS LAST INSPECTION.
	Any aspects that are particularly good or need to improve should be reported under WHAT THE SCHOOL DOES WELL and WHAT COULD BE IMPROVED.
SHORT INSPECTIONS	Expand your judgements in the commentary on matters listed in WHAT THE SCHOOL DOES WELL or WHAT COULD BE IMPROVED.
FULL INSPECTIONS	Report on overall quality and, particularly, on curricular strengths and weaknesses under the heading HOW GOOD ARE THE CURRICULAR AND OTHER OPPORTUNITIES OFFERED TO PUPILS?

GUIDANCE ON USING THE CRITERIA

☐ **The quality and range of opportunities for learning provided by the school, including extra-curricular activities**

☐ **The extent to which the school meets statutory requirements, including provision of religious education where appropriate**

Does the school provide a broad range of worthwhile opportunities which meet the interests, aptitudes and particular needs of pupils, including those having special educational needs?

Before the inspection you should refer to *Form S3* to check whether or not the school is meeting the statutory requirements for the curriculum. Section D2 of *Form S2* will enable you to evaluate how the school allocates the time available to the different subjects of the curriculum. Your evaluation of the breadth and quality of the provision requires you to consider how the school has made decisions about what will be included in the curriculum, and the time allocated to different aspects, taking account of:

■ the National Curriculum and syllabus requirements;

■ the current guidance from the Qualifications and Curriculum Authority;

■ the best use of the specialist skills of staff;

■ the organisation of the school day;

■ suitability of provision for the range of sixth formers, especially GCE courses, GNVQs and other work-related provision;

■ how the school ensures that the needs of all pupils are met and that they have equal access to all areas of the curriculum and opportunities to succeed in them.

In applying the principle of challenge within the best value framework, the school should have a rationale for why the curriculum has been planned in the way it has. In particular, you should explore how the balance of the statutory curriculum has been arrived at and why, particularly, specific non-statutory elements have been included. This is especially relevant in respect of courses provided in Key Stage 4 and the sixth form.

The curriculum in secondary schools is usually organised into separate subjects taught by specialist teachers, but other forms of organisation may be used, for example in relation to vocational courses. Provision for curricular elements such as ICT and health education may be organised in a variety of ways.

In most schools, Key Stage 4 provides the first opportunity for pupils to exercise choice over their curriculum and may feature different types of provision for different groups of pupils as permitted by the National Curriculum. It may be important to establish if different patterns of choice have an ethnic dimension and the reasons for this.

Exploring the extent to which the school has consulted staff, governors, parents and, where appropriate, pupils about its provision will support your judgement about the application of the best value principles in HOW WELL IS THE SCHOOL LED AND MANAGED?

You should find out from *Form S1* the number of pupils on the register of SEN at each stage of the Code of Practice, and what range of needs is represented. When there is a designated unit or resource base, find out whether pupils are grouped together or taught in their appropriate year group classes, in case you need to do extra checks on the curriculum they receive. Find out also how pupils with SEN are organised, for example in withdrawal groups, in-class support or setting, as the arrangements may make a difference to the curriculum pupils receive.

Judge how well the curriculum is organised to meet the needs of pupils with special educational needs. Check that the arrangements for using IEPs are effective in ensuring that individual needs are addressed whilst enabling pupils to have full access to the curriculum. There are likely to be specific arrangements to provide extra help for pupils in literacy and numeracy and other communication skills, and for some of the pupils, help in gaining independence and mobility training or extra help for those who are disturbed and need counselling. For pupils with statements, check that the provision in their statements is implemented in a representative sample by age and disability. In designated units or resource bases judge whether pupils' specific programmes are met, whether by the class teacher in the base or by the arrangements the school makes in all classes, for example in ensuring that pupils have full access to the classroom or by the provision of large print for pupils with visual disability. Assess how well pupils in the unit are integrated in all aspects of the life of the school and whether the curricular arrangements promote inclusion of all pupils with SEN.

Schools with sixth forms

In evaluating the **suitability of the sixth form curriculum,** the most important criterion is whether or not the opportunities provided meet the needs and aspirations of the students recruited. Whilst most sixth forms will provide both GCE AS/A level and GNVQ courses, there may be circumstances where it is appropriate to offer only AS/A levels or only GNVQs. In these cases, however, alternative types of course would need to be available in other post-16 institutions in the area, to allow students an appropriate range of choice.

A few schools offer the International Baccalaureate (IB) for some or all of their advanced level students, or GCSE courses for one-year students. The same criteria for evaluation apply to these as to GCE AS/A levels and GNVQ courses.

Evaluation should also cover the quality and range of the sixth form curriculum beyond that which leads to accreditation in individual subjects or courses. Provision for 'additional' or 'enrichment' studies varies widely between schools. Normally it should encompass the statutory provision of religious education, as well as sport and recreational activities, and careers education and guidance. It may additionally include key skills, A level or AS general studies, personal, social and health education, ICT and community service. It is important that there is a clear and sound rationale for this additional provision.

The success or otherwise of students on different types of sixth form examination courses should provide a pointer to the appropriateness of the sixth form curriculum, and to the effectiveness of guidance in Year 11.

You should also come to a view about the cost-effectiveness of sixth form provision. This requires you to estimate the degree of match between the resources which accrue to the school on the basis of the number of pupils 11–16 and 16+ and the ratio of providing the 'main school' to sixth form provision, in terms of teacher periods. You should take into account the numbers of students who benefit, the distance of alternative provision and the quality of what is offered, when judging the cost-effectiveness of the sixth form. All inspection contractors have been provided with software to assist with the calculation. One key question is the extent to which one part of the school 'subsidises' the provision made in another part.

Example 4.1

Extract from an inspection report: curriculum

The school offers a rich and varied curriculum in the sixth form, with a significant increase in the number of subjects since the last inspection. Teaching is organised jointly with the partner high school. Twenty subjects are offered at A level with nearly half offering the alternative of AS levels. Further mathematics is available in Year 13. Two subjects are offered at GNVQ advanced and four at intermediate levels. There are opportunities for students to re-sit GCSE English and mathematics. All students following A level and advanced GNVQ courses take the A level general studies course that includes a strand entitled 'Values' which is effective in teaching religious education. But statutory requirements for students following GNVQ intermediate courses are not fully met. Personal and careers guidance is provided through an individual tutorial system which is valued by students and which is most effective. A post-16 careers adviser, based in the sixth form centre, has excellent academic and personal knowledge of the individual students, who value her encyclopaedic knowledge of career opportunities and higher education entry requirements.

[Overall: sixth form curriculum very good (2)]

Does the school have effective strategies for teaching the basic skills of literacy and numeracy?

Many schools already follow aspects of the National Literacy Strategy and the National Numeracy Strategy in Key Stage 3. Where this is so you will need to evaluate how effective they are in raising standards. In reaching this judgement you must take account of the results the school achieves in National Curriculum tests and any other assessments at Key Stage 3. Where they do not, you will need to evaluate what the school has done to improve standards of literacy and numeracy.

Does the school provide enrichment through its extra-curricular provision, including support for learning outside the school day?

The effective school will make arrangements to help all pupils take advantage of opportunities to learn, for example by visits out of school, running after-school homework clubs and extra-curricular activities at different times of the day so that all pupils who wish to can attend. Schools often provide a good range of extra-curricular activities, including competitive sport, music, drama, community work, foreign exchanges, theatre visits and homework classes. Effective schools will plan this provision and monitor and evaluate its contribution to attainment and attitudes. The opportunity to take part and the number of pupils involved in all such activities will contribute to your evaluation. Your report should make explicit reference to the quality of study support and provision of sport.

Is the curriculum socially inclusive by ensuring equality of access and opportunity for all pupils?

You need to make sure that you have accurately recorded the groups of pupils who form the intake of the school in THE CHARACTERISTICS OF THE SCHOOL. Once you have defined the groups, check your preliminary analysis of performance and take-up of courses to see if there are any significant differences in the attainment, experience and benefit gained from what the school provides. You can then set some initial hypotheses for the inspection which you can test out through your observations, work sampling and discussions with pupils. When you have gathered the evidence, evaluate the extent to which:

- all pupils benefit according to need from what the school provides;

- any groups of pupils do not do as well as others and if the school is aware of this;

- the school offers justifiable explanations for any differences;

- the school has taken effective action if needed.

☐ **For FULL INSPECTIONS only, the school's provision for personal, social and health education, careers education and guidance and citizenship and the quality of the school's links with the community and other schools, colleges and initial teacher training consortia**

The four evaluations that relate to this overarching question only apply to FULL INSPECTIONS. However, you can acquire much of the evidence you need to make these judgements on both SHORT and FULL INSPECTIONS. These judgements will help you evaluate how well the school prepares its pupils for adult life in partnership with others.

Does the school provide effectively for personal and social education, including health education, sex education and attention to drug misuse and citizenship?

Schools must promote the spiritual, moral, social and cultural, mental and physical development of pupils at the school and prepare them for the opportunities, responsibilities and experiences of adult life.

This is achieved through the ethos of the school, its curriculum, its extra-curricular provision and its provision for the spiritual, moral, social and cultural development of its pupils. The intended outcomes of the provision are often clearly stated in the aims of the school. Other aspects of personal and social development occur when a school responds to the individual needs of pupils.

These may be difficult to predict and plan for, but an effective school will respond either through its own pupil support systems or by engaging with the appropriate external agencies.

Personal, Social and Health Education (PSHE) promotes the personal and social development of its pupils. This will be provided through discrete lessons as well as through opportunities provided by the subjects of the National Curriculum, assemblies, the tutorial programme, work experience and mini-enterprise schemes, guidance and support systems, special projects and other events which enrich pupils' experiences.

A broad and balanced PSHE curriculum will encompass aspects of health, including sex education and drug education; environmental education; economic and industrial understanding; careers education and guidance; citizenship. PSHE programmes will also contribute to the development of communication, problem-solving and inter-personal skills.

Does the school provide effectively for work-related education, including careers education and guidance?

You should evaluate how far pupils have opportunities to learn 'about work', 'through work' and 'for work'. You will have to ensure that the inspection team is deployed in such a way that, as far as possible, work-related aspects of the curriculum are inspected and evidence co-ordinated.

You should evaluate:

- the quality of the curriculum and the extent to which it prepares pupils for the next stage of education;

- the contribution made by school–business partnerships, vocational education, training or employment;

- the contribution made by school subjects and extra-curricular activities;

- how the use of specific resources supports work-related learning;

- the standards of key skills taught (communication, application of number and information technology);

- the quality of teaching and its impact on educational standards achieved.

Further detailed guidance is provided in *Inspecting Subjects and Aspects 11–18: Work-Related Education and Careers Education and Guidance*.

Does the school have links with the community which contribute to pupils' learning?

Many schools see themselves as part of the community they serve. You will need to assess the sort of links the school has established and with whom and ask if the school has done all it can to contribute to the range of communities represented by the pupils in the school and to tap the resources available within its locality and beyond. Access to the Internet and well-developed skills in information and communication technology mean that many pupils now have enriching opportunities to link with others all around the world.

Your evaluation should centre on the contribution made to pupils' intellectual and personal development by the school's involvement with, and contribution to, the community. There may be links with a range of organisations, services and employers which help pupils to gain an understanding of society, citizenship and the world of work. Some of these links may set teaching in a work-related context.

Formal community education will be part of provision in many schools. You will need to determine how far it serves both the community and the school, bringing local experience in and using the school as a formal and informal resource for learning and for the development of the community.

You must consider:

- how far the purposes of community education link with the aims of the school;

- whether direction and leadership are clear and supportive;

- how far the range of provision is based on a systematic analysis of need;

- how far the impact of the provision in the school and the community is monitored.

Does the school have constructive relationships with partner institutions such as link schools?

A school with good links with its partner institutions will, at age 11 (or 12, 13, 14, if there are middle schools):

- draw on and use what the primary schools know about the pupils' attainment;

- collect and use a range of information about pupils' attitudes, values and personal development;

- be clear about pupils' strengths and weaknesses in literacy and numeracy, particularly for those pupils with special educational needs;

- familiarise pupils and parents with the expectations and pattern of work of secondary education before they are on the roll;

at age 16:

- provide pupils with a survey of their academic and personal achievements as a basis for their future choices;

- provide consistent and impartial advice on what comes next, based on a good knowledge of what is available;

- keep track of the choices and the progress students make;

at age 18:

- take care to assemble its knowledge of the range and variety of post-18 opportunities, including employment;

- provide students with good-quality advice and guidance on future choices, on an individual basis.

☐ **How well the school cultivates pupils' personal – including spiritual, moral, social and cultural – development**

Does the school provide pupils with knowledge and insights into values and beliefs, and enable them to reflect on their experiences in a way which develops their spiritual awareness and self-knowledge?

Effective provision for spiritual development depends on a curriculum and approaches to teaching which embody clear values and provide opportunities for pupils to gain understanding by developing a sense of curiosity through reflection on their own and other people's lives and beliefs. It relies on teachers receiving and valuing pupils' ideas across the whole curriculum, for example in literature, art, music, history and religious education. Acts of collective worship play a particular part. To the extent that spiritual insights imply an awareness of how pupils relate to others, there is a strong link to both moral and social development.

Although religious education and spiritual development are not synonymous, religious education can make a significant contribution to spiritual development. You might consider, for example, whether pupils are encouraged to:

■ consider life's fundamental questions and how religious teaching can relate to them;

■ respond to such questions with reference to the teachings and practices of religions as well as from their own experience and viewpoint;

■ reflect on their own beliefs or values in the light of what they are studying in religious education.

Collective worship

You should evaluate collective worship in all schools which do not provide denominational education. Evaluation should focus on whether acts of worship are well planned and encourage pupils to explore questions about meaning and purpose, values and beliefs. Compliance with statutory requirements on collective worship should be recorded in *Form S3*.

The law requires schools other than Pupil Referral Units to provide a daily act of collective worship. Taken over a term, the majority of such acts of worship should be wholly or mainly of a broadly Christian character. The school prospectus should make clear the parents' right to withdraw their children from collective worship. In forming a judgement about the character and quality of worship in schools, the following points may be helpful:

■ worship is generally understood to imply the recognition of a supreme being. It should be clear that the words used and/or the activities observed in worship recognise the existence of a deity;

■ collective worship should not be judged by the presence or absence of a particular ingredient. It might include: sharing values of a Christian nature; opportunities for prayers or meditation; opportunities to reflect upon readings from holy texts or other writings which bring out religious themes; and performance of music, drama and/or dance;

■ each act of worship in a school should be considered for its individual qualities. However, before reaching a judgement about the activities observed during the inspection they should be set alongside the evidence of what has occurred, and is planned, over a term. On balance, if it is judged that what the school provides is not in keeping with the spirit of the law, then this should be recorded and explained;

■ worship may be judged not to fulfil statutory requirements but could still be observed to make a powerful contribution to pupils' spiritual, moral, social and cultural development. That should be made clear in the report.

Does the school promote principles which distinguish right from wrong?

The essence of moral development is to build a framework of values which regulate personal behaviour. It is done through teaching and promoting principles rather than through fear of punishment or reward. Pupils are able to make moral decisions but their learning about moral issues may be on a different plane from their behaviour. Moral and social education are closely related and depend on the school fostering values such as honesty, fairness and respect for truth and justice.

You should consider whether the school provides a moral code as a basis for behaviour which is promoted through the life of the school. You should also look at the opportunities for pupils to develop and express moral values and extend social and personal understanding across a range of issues, including, for example, personal rights and responsibilities, and equal opportunities.

Does the school encourage pupils to take responsibility, show initiative and develop an understanding of living in a community?

Social development hinges on an acceptance of group rules and the ability to set oneself in a wider context. Adolescents may find that the need to be socially compliant is sometimes at odds with their developing moral sensibility. Partly for this reason, the quality of relationships in schools is of crucial importance in forming pupils' attitudes to good social behaviour and self-discipline.

You need to consider how the school, through its organisation, curriculum and other activities, contributes to social development through experience and understanding of social relationships and the rights and responsibilities of individuals within the social setting. Evidence may include opportunities for pupils to work co-operatively in lessons, on projects or in games involving competition, discipline and fair play. You should take account of opportunities for pupils to take on responsibility, demonstrate initiative and contribute to the life of the school as a community. Vocational courses at Key Stage 4 and post-16 can play a significant part in this development.

Does the school teach the pupils to appreciate their own cultural traditions as well as the diversity and richness of other cultures?

The school's approach should be active. You need to look for evidence of how the school seeks to enrich its pupils' knowledge and experience of their own and other cultural traditions of the area where the school is set and the ethnic and cultural diversity of British society. Aspects of the curriculum in all subjects can contribute positively, for example through opportunities for pupils to:

- visit museums, art galleries, theatres, cinemas and concerts;

- work with artists, authors and performers;

- develop open and enquiring attitudes towards the music and dance of different cultures;

- appreciate the natural world through art, literature, science and mathematics;

- recognise the contribution of many cultures to mathematics and to scientific and technological development.

5. HOW WELL DOES THE SCHOOL CARE FOR ITS PUPILS OR STUDENTS?

Inspectors must evaluate and report on:

- ☐ the steps taken to ensure pupils' welfare, health and safety, including the school's arrangements for child protection;

- ☐ the effectiveness of the school's assessment and monitoring of pupils' academic performance, and monitoring of personal development and attendance;

- ☐ the effectiveness of the school's educational and personal support and guidance in raising pupils' achievements.

In determining their judgements, inspectors should consider the extent to which the school:

- ensures the health, safety, care and protection of all pupils and students;

- has effective measures to promote good attendance and behaviour, and to eliminate oppressive behaviour including all forms of harassment and bullying;

- has effective arrangements for assessing pupils' attainments and progress;

- uses its assessment information to guide its planning;

- provides effective support and advice for all its pupils, informed by the monitoring of their academic progress, personal development, behaviour and attendance.

INSPECTION FOCUS

Focus your inspection on the effectiveness of the care taken by the school for pupils, whatever their needs or circumstances, not just on the policies and systems. There are three components to the inspection of care and guidance:

- the welfare and safety and child protection arrangements for pupils;

- the assessment of pupils' academic and personal development, as well as their attendance;

- the use of support and guidance to raise pupils' achievement.

Although much of the evidence you gather will be common to all three components, in SHORT INSPECTIONS you are only required to make judgements and report on the first of these, *unless* concerns emerge about the care of pupils. If you are concerned, you must explore these further.

In all inspections:

- give priority to pupils' safety and protection, and report on any aspect of care which is a strength or weakness in your report summary and commentary;

- always report orally any shortcomings in health and safety matters to the governors. Do not publish any information that could jeopardise pupils' safety.

If pupils are not well cared for they will not be able to learn effectively. There are particularly vulnerable young people that the school needs to protect, for example those with special educational needs, those who are shy and withdrawn, and those who are known to be at risk.

From your pre-inspection analysis and initial visit, you already know some of the challenges and issues the school faces. These will give a specific focus to your inspection.

MAKING JUDGEMENTS

In SHORT INSPECTIONS, make sure you take account of all the relevant criteria to come to your judgements about whether pupils' welfare is safeguarded, even though you are not required to report on them. This ensures that all aspects of welfare are considered.

The following characteristics illustrate where to pitch your judgements about how well the school cares for its pupils.

Very good or excellent	Teachers know individual pupils very well, including those from particular groups or with SEN, and are fully aware of their physical, emotional and intellectual needs. They respond to them in a positive and supportive way. The day-to-day work of the school, in terms of supervision, awareness of hazard and the promotion of healthy living, creates a strong sense of the importance of health and safety of pupils. The school has effective practices in place to identify how well pupils are making progress, particularly in the core subjects, and the achievements of different groups. This identification is followed by good diagnosis of what such groups do well and how they might improve. The school has systematic and effective ways of being aware of developing patterns in pupils' behaviour or attendance and relating these to patterns of achievement. The systematic monitoring of pupils leads to changes or modifications to the curriculum, for example, or to individual support for pupils' performance and development.
Satisfactory or better	Teachers know pupils well, recognise their needs and respond well to them. The working environment is safe and pupils are properly supervised. The school maintains records of pupils' achievements in most aspects of the core curriculum and individual action plans are in place and used for pupils with special education needs to monitor progress and guide teaching. The school promotes good behaviour and attendance through agreed, shared and successfully implemented policies. The monitoring of pupils' performance and development is used to make changes in approach and emphasis.

The school's care of its pupils **cannot be satisfactory** if:

- it does not take reasonable steps to ensure the care of individual pupils and minimise the possibility of harm;

- it does not have satisfactory arrangements to track the progress of pupils across the subjects and courses they study, and take action to raise achievement;

- it does not adequately monitor and deal with problems of behaviour and attendance.

REPORTING REQUIREMENTS

SUMMARY REPORT	On all inspections you must complete the box, HOW WELL DOES THE SCHOOL CARE FOR ITS PUPILS OR STUDENTS?, in the table headed OTHER ASPECTS OF THE SCHOOL with comments on any particular strengths and weaknesses.
	If any of these are a feature of improvement in the school, record this in the section HOW THE SCHOOL HAS IMPROVED SINCE ITS LAST INSPECTION.
	Any aspects that are particularly good or need to improve should be reported under WHAT THE SCHOOL DOES WELL or WHAT COULD BE IMPROVED.
SHORT INSPECTIONS	Expand in the commentary any parts from WHAT THE SCHOOL DOES WELL and WHAT COULD BE IMPROVED.
FULL INSPECTIONS	Report under the heading HOW WELL DOES THE SCHOOL CARE FOR ITS PUPILS OR STUDENTS?

GUIDANCE ON USING THE CRITERIA

☐ **The steps taken to ensure pupils' welfare and safety, including the school's arrangements for child protection**

Does the school ensure the health, safety, care and protection of all pupils?

The quality of care is evident in *all* the relationships in the school, in teachers' knowledge of children and their needs and how the school acts to promote the best interests of all individual pupils.

Pupils' welfare and safety are reflected in the quality of care they receive and the effectiveness of the school's arrangements to:

- ensure that each child is well known by at least one teacher, who links effectively with staff with key responsibilities in the school;

- ensure that all children and staff work in a safe environment;

- ensure child protection arrangements comply with procedures that are agreed locally;

- promote good attendance;

- promote good behaviour which is free from harassment and bullying;

- identify and meet individual needs, including those of pupils with special educational needs;

- promote healthy and safe living;

- ensure that work-related opportunities conform to health and safety criteria.

In ALL INSPECTIONS, the data provided by the school will give you a starting point for your further investigations. For example, the data on attendance and exclusions, and information from the headteacher's statement in *Form S4,* will give you important indicators.

When you walk around the school judge the safety of the environment for pupils and staff:

- ask about the day-to-day working practices to ensure that pupils and staff are protected from harm;

- check that the health and safety policy is regularly monitored;

- check the quality of supervision during break and before and after school.

Good schools will successfully build on their day-to-day arrangements in complying with procedures adopted by the local Area Child Protection Committee (ACPC). You should check whether:

- staff are aware who the designated senior member of staff responsible is;

- the school policy is in line with local procedures;

- staff are aware of what to do if they suspect, or have disclosed to them, that an individual pupil may need protection;

- the designated member of staff has detailed knowledge of local procedures;

- staff know who the LEA responsible officer is;

- staff have knowledge of the possible signs and symptoms of child abuse;

- new staff are informed about what to do as part of their induction;

- all staff receive in-service training to maintain and update their knowledge and understanding of procedures.

Find out how the school liaises with other agencies in monitoring the progress of pupils on the 'at risk' register. For example, find out the arrangements for attending case conferences and for providing reports at the request of the ACPC on how individual children are getting on at school. In addition you will find evidence in the school's curriculum to judge how the pupils are helped to look after themselves and to develop a responsible attitude as they grow up. If you find a school does not have effective procedures complying with those of the ACPC, explain any mis-match when it occurs. This must be reported to the headteacher and the governing body and included in the inspection report.

You will need to evaluate how successfully the school cares for pupils who are known to need particular attention and for whom the school needs to be especially vigilant. The school has a duty, for example, to ensure that the provision outlined in statements of SEN is implemented. The provision may require liaison with external SEN support staff and other agencies such as health authorities and social services departments. Other pupils with dietary or medical problems, or difficult home circumstances, may require the school to take particular care. Find out how well aware the school is of any pupils 'looked after' by the local authority, and how sensitively staff who need to know the particular circumstances liaise with carers.

In an effective school, staff will know in detail about the different needs of pupils and will provide consistent and convincing responses to your questions about what they do to help pupils, and how pupils are helped to look after themselves. Look at the impact the personal, social and health education programme has in helping pupils to be increasingly independent, self-confident and knowledgeable about themselves and healthy and safe living. If the school is part of the government's 'healthy school' initiative you should be able to trace and evaluate the impact of this participation in the day-to-day work of the school.

Example 5.1

Extract from an inspection report: health and safety

There are sound policies and broadly satisfactory practice on health and safety. The safety equipment is checked periodically and the procedures for reporting, recording and investigating accidents are fully implemented. The school nurse ensures that all health and safety matters are dealt with promptly and efficiently. However, during the inspection two health and safety issues were identified: some fire doors were locked and thus posed a potential danger to the school community; and some staff in the physical education department did not undertake appropriate precautions to ensure fully the safety of pupils using the trampoline.

[Overall: health and safety unsatisfactory (5)]

Does the school have effective measures to promote good attendance and behaviour, and to eliminate oppressive behaviour such as all forms of harassment and bullying?

The priority staff give to encouraging good attendance and behaviour is a strong indicator of the steps taken by the school to ensure pupils' welfare and safety. Do teachers encourage individual pupils to attend and be punctual, and is this backed up in assemblies, which are often occasions when the whole school is reminded about attendance? You may have picked up from the parents' questionnaire, or at the meeting before the inspection, how the school encourages parents to ensure their child's attendance.

The responsibility for reminding pupils about how to behave well, and about their attitudes to others, rests with all teachers. Look at the evidence from HOW WELL ARE PUPILS TAUGHT? which tells you how successfully teachers minimise disruption and poor behaviour through their skilful handling of pupils in lessons and help pupils know what behaviour is expected of them. You should assess the impact of the school's statutory behaviour policy in promoting respect and tolerance towards others and their beliefs, cultures and ethnic backgrounds.

Check that the policy makes clear the school's intolerance of bullying and racial and sexual harassment. Check that policies for recording the pattern and frequency of racial incidents are in place and that such incidents and the actions taken are reported annually to the governing body, parents and the LEA. See how consistently staff reward pupils for good work and behaviour in and outside the school, and, when there is poor behaviour, that sanctions are also consistently and appropriately used in proportion to the misdemeanours.

Your observations around the school, in lessons, and in discussions with pupils will help you evaluate how the school eliminates oppressive behaviour, bullying and harassment. Ask for the records of any incidents that have taken place during the previous 12 months and take particular note of the measures the school takes to prevent bullying, harassment and racial incidents, and decide whether, in your view, they are working. Check that no groups or individuals are unfairly treated or disadvantaged.

Example 5.2

Unsatisfactory support and guidance

The school's response to unsatisfactory behaviour in lessons from a dozen or so boys in the three lower ability sets in Y9 has been inconsistent and piecemeal. Some teachers have taken the use of a room where pupils could be sent during lessons if their behaviour disrupted the work of others as too easy a solution. This has resulted in grouping together the same pupils in this withdrawal room and has increased the potential for yet further poor behaviour. The lack of senior staff supervision for this room has led to much loss of impact on the pupils concerned. This, coupled with the fact that there is no consistent approach about what work pupils should do when withdrawn from the mainstream lesson, has meant that the behaviour of difficult pupils has deteriorated and there has been a marked decline, as seen from their books, both in the quality of their work and the amount they complete.

☐ **The effectiveness of the school's assessment and monitoring of pupils' academic performance, and monitoring of their personal development and attendance**

Does the school have effective arrangements for assessing pupils' attainments and progress? Does it use its assessment information to guide its planning?

In FULL INSPECTIONS you should evaluate how effective the school is in assessing how well pupils are doing academically and how well they are developing in their personal skills.

The school's practice in assessment needs to be seen in relation to:

■ the assessment requirements of the National Curriculum at the end of Key Stage 2 (for middle/deemed secondary schools) and Key Stage 3;

■ public examination requirements at Key Stage 4 and post-16;

■ the requirements covering pupil records and reports, including annual reports to parents and reports to school leavers;

■ the use and compilation of the National Record of Achievement;

■ the additional requirements which apply to pupils with statements of special educational needs and those at the earlier stages of the Code of Practice;

■ the support needs of EAL learners and the integration of any additional assessments with the school's normal assessment procedures.

You should judge how well teachers assess pupils in all aspects of their work, behaviour and personal development so that they have a full picture of their pupils' strengths and weaknesses. This should include qualities such as persistence, application, co-operation with others, ability to concentrate, and self-confidence. See if the teacher assesses how well individual pupils behave in different contexts, for example in lessons where pupils are encouraged to investigate individually or in groups, or in physical education and sports. Check how well heads of department and assessment co-ordinators work together with teachers so that consistent records are produced and used throughout the school to guide planning and improve achievement.

See how effectively the school builds on its assessment procedures when identifying pupils with SEN to comply with the Code of Practice. Judge how effective and consistent the procedures are for placing pupils on the register and for deciding what further help is needed in accordance with the school's SEN policy and the guidance in the Code.

Judge how well the school monitors the results of its assessments so as to identify the achievements of different ethnic groups by ability or by gender. Check how well this information is recorded and analysed (particularly in providing support for EAL) to help the school take action to improve achievement. If there is no evidence of monitoring the achievement of different groups of pupils, it raises questions about how effective the school is in meeting the needs of all the pupils.

Look at how the school monitors its attendance and analyses the attendance data. See that teachers understand what constitutes authorised absence and how consistent they are in recording unauthorised absence.

Judge how well the behaviour policy is reviewed if exclusions take place, and whether the governing body is properly involved, and what action the school takes to amend its practice, if necessary. Parents should be kept informed about the behaviour policy at least annually.

☐ The effectiveness of a school's educational and personal support and guidance in raising pupils' achievements

Does the school provide effective support and advice for all its pupils, informed by the monitoring of their academic progress, personal development, behaviour and attendance?

In FULL INSPECTIONS, your judgement on how effectively the school supports pupils to raise their achievements relies on what you have already found out about assessment practice and the use made of assessment. See what the school does to acknowledge pupils' achievements, particularly when great strides in progress have taken place. Evaluate the effect this has on encouraging all pupils to achieve more.

Find out and assess how well the school identifies what action it can take to help individuals or groups of pupils, for example through changes to the day-to-day organisation and through the provision of extra help. See how well the school discusses what it knows about pupils' strengths and weaknesses with pupils themselves, and with parents and other agencies. Assess how carefully the school deals with pupils who need to improve their skills and how, in liaison with parents, they are encouraged, yet challenged, to improve.

If targets are set for individual pupils do they focus only on attainment or also on other specific aspects of their life at school, such as their behaviour or attendance? Check that the targets are clear and can be monitored for success. Assess if the school strikes the right balance between doing the best it can, within its resources, before asking for outside help. Make sure the school discriminates between those occasions where outside agencies must be asked for help (for example, child protection) and where it is reasonable for the school to provide support internally.

Does the school meet the statutory requirements for day and residential provision as outlined in statements of special educational needs?

Your pre-inspection work on the characteristics of the school should alert you to those pupils who have statements of SEN. Evidence from the section on HOW GOOD ARE THE CURRICULAR AND OTHER OPPORTUNITIES OFFERED TO PUPILS? should help you in making this judgement. You should make sure that you scrutinise pupils' statements; all of them when there are five or less, and no less than half when numbers are greater, so that a representative sample by age and disability is looked at. You should check that the statements or reviews are up to date so that you know that the provision outlined in the statement is implemented by the school and any other agency involved, such as speech therapists or LEA support staff. Any evident shortfall in the provision should be further checked to find out why this is so. Ensure that specific disability-related provision is implemented, such as aids for hearing, seeing, writing or to facilitate mobility or for specific arrangements in respect of personal hygiene. Check that access to additional staffing indicated in the statement is in place and used effectively. Make sure that specific curricular arrangements are met such as work in literacy, numeracy and oracy and that, overall, pupils have their entitlement to a broad and balanced curriculum. Check that arrangements specified in the statement for ensuring that pupils have full access to the whole of the school's curriculum are in place. Where residential provision is specified, check that the arrangements provided by the school match the statement, particularly in respect of the number of nights boarding, regularity of contact with pupils' parents or carers, and specified programmes, for example to boost independence or self-care skills. You need to be sure that suitable arrangements are in place to enable all key members of staff who need to know the provision are aware of the contents of the statement and are able subsequently to contribute to any review that takes place. Attend if possible an annual or transition review to ensure that the provision is re-examined in the light of any progress made and that key people attend as appropriate.

Do the care arrangements for boarding pupils take account of the Children Act 1989?

If the contract requires inspection of boarding provision, you must evaluate how effectively:

- the school safeguards pupils' welfare and protects them from harm in the residential setting;

- the school supports childcare staff to plan for individual pupils;

- the school helps individual pupils to develop emotionally, socially and physically so they can benefit educationally;

- the school provides arrangements for study support and 'home' work;

- the school provides healthy and nutritious food and looks after pupils' medical needs;

- the school protects pupils by the vetting and supervision of staff, and the provision of well-understood and effective arrangements for pupils to complain, and to have direct and unfettered access to outside help if required;

- pupils have sufficient privacy, appropriate to age and needs, in well-maintained and suitable accommodation;

- pupils have regular opportunities to make personal choices, for example in their clothing and leisure activities.

You should check that the ethos of the boarding provision is such that pupils feel secure, valued and respected as individuals and are able to thrive. Relationships between pupils and pupils, and between staff and pupils should reflect this ethos. Opportunities should be available for pupils to gain in self-esteem by the provision of planned activities and opportunities to gain independence. They should be helped to show concern for others and to accept responsibility as they grow older, in preparation for adult life. You should check that the use of sanctions and rewards is appropriate to the pupils and is consistent and fair in its implementation. You should check that staffing levels are sufficient to provide the necessary supervision and support, according to needs. Where appropriate, provision should be available for drugs and sex education, and in dealing with the consequences of sexual and other physical or emotional abuse. Staffing should be sufficient to promote links with families and other important people in pupils' lives, particularly when they live some distance from the school or stay at school for most of the year.

6. HOW WELL DOES THE SCHOOL WORK IN PARTNERSHIP WITH PARENTS ?

Inspectors must evaluate and report on:

☐ parents' views of the school;

☐ the effectiveness of the school's links with parents;

☐ the impact of the parents' involvement with the work of the school.

In determining their judgements, inspectors should consider the extent to which:

• parents are satisfied with what the school provides and achieves;

• parents are provided with good quality information about the school, and particularly about pupils' progress;

• links with parents, including the use of home–school agreements, contribute to pupils' learning at school and at home.

INSPECTION FOCUS

Parents depend on the school to provide well for their sons and daughters. You need to find out whether they feel the school lives up to their expectations and responds to any concerns.

Where a school uses the OFSTED parents' questionnaire you will be able to evaluate how parents feel about the main aspects of the school. You need to use your professional judgement as to the number of responses to a question that signify an important strength or weakness as perceived by parents. The responses to the questionnaire will indicate where you may need more information and issues you may want to follow up at the parents' meeting.

The best opportunity for parents to share their views with you comes at the meeting for parents who have children at the school. You must use this meeting:

- to explore the views of parents on those aspects of the school specified in the inspection schedule;

- to follow up issues from the parents' responses to the questionnaire;

- to allow parents to tell you what they think about the school;

- to judge whether there are groups of parents who have not been heard and provide an opportunity for their views to be heard.

There are many other opportunities for you to find out what parents think of the school. For instance:

- parents may ask to see you or speak to you on the telephone during an inspection;

- talking with parents who work and help in the school;

- there may be an event for parents during the period of the inspection, which an inspector should visit.

On SHORT INSPECTIONS, you are only required to follow up the areas relating to issues raised by parents' views that seem from the parents' meeting and questionnaire to be important.

On FULL INSPECTIONS, evaluate also how well the school involves parents as partners in their children's learning; the quality and effectiveness of the information it provides for parents, and particularly the effect these have on improving pupils' achievements, including their personal development.

Evaluate how well the school consults parents about its curricular provision and about major spending decisions. This will tell you about the application of the principle of consultation within the best value framework.

MAKING JUDGEMENTS

To make your judgements, use all the evidence you have about the parents' level of satisfaction with the school, the effectiveness of the school's partnership with them and the contribution that this partnership makes to pupils' learning.

Consider this evidence alongside the evidence and judgements that you have made in HOW WELL DOES THE SCHOOL CARE FOR ITS PUPILS? In particular, examine those judgements you have made on the effectiveness of support and advice provided by the school for its pupils and how well parents are able to use this information to help their children learn.

The following characteristics illustrate where to pitch judgements about how well the school works in partnership with parents and carers.

Very good or excellent	The school has a very good range of productive and consistent links with parents that help pupils learn. The mechanisms for exchanging information between school and home are effective and include opportunities for parents to give information to the school about their son or daughter. Information to parents through written reports is of good quality, making clear what pupils need to do to improve and how parents can help. There is strong parental satisfaction within the school, based on secure understanding and regular involvement in its work. There should be clear improvement in pupils' learning, behaviour and personal development resulting from good liaison with parents.
Satisfactory or better	The school has effective links with parents to support pupils' learning. Parents are, in the main, satisfied with the standards achieved and what the school provides, with no major concerns. Reports to parents are clear and useful, and the exchange of information is sound.

However, the partnership with parents **cannot be satisfactory** if:

- there is a significant degree of dissatisfaction among parents about the school's work, which is supported by inspection findings;

- information to parents does not give a clear view of pupils' progress;

- parents are kept at arm's length and the school makes little effort to communicate with them and involve them in the life of the school.

Example 6.1

Extract from an inspection report: parents and the school

Since the last inspection the school has made substantial and successful efforts to adapt the curriculum at Key Stage 4 in the light of parents' demands for much greater flexibility of courses, particularly the opportunities for work-related approaches. Parents have been extensively consulted on new GNVQ areas of work and there has been a series of well-attended meetings for parents with experts in GNVQ and teachers from other schools, where these courses have been introduced successfully. Parents reported a very much improved level of information about the nature of these courses and what they offered for future study and for work. Standards of work seen in these areas of Key Stage 4 are high, reflecting the strength of the home–school commitment to the new opportunities offered.

[Very good involvement of and links with parents (2)]

REPORTING REQUIREMENTS

SUMMARY REPORT	All inspectors must complete the table headed PARENTS' VIEWS OF THE SCHOOLS, and state the extent to which the inspection team agrees with parents' views. If the school's work with parents is a feature of improvement in the school, record this in the section HOW THE SCHOOL HAS IMPROVED SINCE ITS LAST INSPECTION. Any aspect that is particularly good or needs to improve should be reported under WHAT THE SCHOOL DOES WELL and WHAT COULD BE IMPROVED.
SHORT INSPECTIONS	Only parents' views of the school are reported. Expand any points made in the commentary under WHAT THE SCHOOL DOES WELL and WHAT COULD BE IMPROVED.
FULL INSPECTIONS	Report under the heading HOW WELL DOES THE SCHOOL WORK IN PARTNERSHIP WITH PARENTS?

GUIDANCE ON USING THE CRITERIA

☐ Parents' views of the school

Are parents satisfied with what the school provides and achieves?

You need to establish how far parents are satisfied with the quality and effectiveness of what the school provides and achieves. Decide whether the inspection evidence supports or refutes the views of parents and why. These judgements must then be reported in the summary and, as appropriate, in the commentary.

On SHORT INSPECTIONS, you are unlikely to have much time for more detailed work on the quality of the partnership between parents and the school, although where you do find evidence, for instance when examining information provided by the school for parents, you may want to take it into account. On SHORT INSPECTIONS, you should only follow up those areas of the school's relationship with parents that seem from the meeting and questionnaire to be burning issues or that shed important light on what the school does well or not so well.

☐ The effectiveness of the school's links with parents

☐ The impact of parents' involvement with the work of the school

Are parents provided with good-quality information about the school, and particularly about pupils' progress?

On a FULL INSPECTION, you must evaluate the effectiveness and impact of the school's partnership with parents. The good school sees parents as a rich resource with an important contribution to make and helps parents to support their children's learning. The way in which the school does this and the extent to which the school and parents work together will have an effect on how well pupils make progress in school.

You must evaluate the extent to which the school actively draws in all parents including those from minority ethnic backgrounds, especially those who do not speak English as a first language, and encourages them to support their children's learning. Your starting point and the source of issues you wish to pursue will be the parents' responses to the questionnaire and their contributions to the parents' meeting. Further evidence will emerge from:

- talking with parents at other times than at the meeting;

- meeting with any parents who work and help in the school;

- talking with parent governors and any representatives from parents' associations and clubs;

- how far information provided for parents can be understood and used;

- how well the school keeps in touch with parents who have little English.

Do links with parents, including the use of home–school agreements, contribute to pupils' learning at school and at home?

An effective partnership includes the sharing of information about pupils, their learning and how they feel about school. Find out whether the induction programmes are flexible enough to suit the needs of all pupils. Examine the effectiveness of arrangements for contacts with pupils' homes, to identify and help pupils who are unhappy, and for involving parents who rarely come to the school.

Assessing the quality of information provided for parents is one part of this evaluation. Examine, for instance:

- any policies on home–school contracts and the extent to which they work;

- how far parents and teachers can talk informally together about pupils, and the arrangements that are made for parents whose first language is not English;

- whether reports to parents about pupils' progress tell them clearly what their children are doing, how well they are doing it, whether it is good enough and what they need to do to improve;

- to what extent written reports are followed up and discussed with parents;

- the extent to which pupils' reports and records incorporate the views of parents and show the action agreed to help pupils learn;

- how well the school helps parents to understand what is taught;

- the extent to which any home–school agreements contribute to pupils' learning;

- whether parents of children with special educational needs are properly involved in identifying their needs, providing appropriate support and regularly reviewing their child's progress;

- how well the school communicates with parents who have disabilities, learning difficulties or who live a long way from school without easy transport;

- how well the school consults parents about its curriculum and about major spending decisions within its application of the consultation principle in the best value framework.

7. HOW WELL IS THE SCHOOL LED AND MANAGED?

Inspectors must evaluate and report on:

- [ ] how efficiently and effectively the headteacher and key staff lead and manage the school, promoting high standards and effective teaching and learning;

- [ ] how well the governing body fulfils its statutory responsibilities and accounts for the performance and improvement of the school;

- [ ] how effectively the school monitors and evaluates its performance, diagnoses its strengths and weaknesses and takes effective action to secure improvements;

- [ ] the extent to which the school makes the best strategic use of its resources, including specific grants and additional funding, linking decisions on spending to educational priorities;

- [ ] the extent to which the principles of best value are applied in the school's use of resources;

- [ ] the adequacy of staffing, accommodation and learning resources, highlighting strengths and weaknesses in different subjects and areas of the curriculum where they affect the quality of education provided and the educational standards achieved.

In determining their judgements, inspectors should consider the extent to which:

- leadership ensures clear direction for the work and development of the school, and promotes high standards;

- the school has explicit aims and values, including a commitment to good relationships and equality of opportunity for all, which are reflected in all its work;

- there is rigorous monitoring, evaluation and development of teaching;

- there is effective appraisal and performance management;

- the school identifies appropriate priorities and targets, takes the necessary action, and reviews progress towards them;

- there is a shared commitment to improvement and the capacity to succeed;

- governors fulfil their statutory duties in helping to shape the direction of the school and have a good understanding of its strengths and weaknesses;

- educational priorities are supported through careful financial management;

- good delegation ensures the effective contribution of staff with management responsibilities;

- effective use is made of new technology, including information and communications technology (ICT);

- specific grant is used effectively for its designated purpose(s);

- the number, qualifications and experience of teachers and support staff match the demands of the curriculum;

- the accommodation allows the curriculum to be taught effectively;

- learning resources are adequate for school's curriculum and range of pupils;

- there is effective induction of staff new to the school and the school is, or has the potential to be, an effective provider of initial teacher training;

- the best value principles of comparison, challenge, consultation and competition are applied in the school's management and use of resources.

INSPECTION FOCUS

Good schools are led and managed for the benefit of all their pupils. Your inspection must focus on the extent to which leadership and management create an effective and improving school where pupils are keen and able to learn. You must evaluate impact rather than intention and ensure that your judgements on the effectiveness of leadership and the efficiency of management make sense when set against your judgements about standards and impact elsewhere in the *Schedule*.

In all inspections focus on:

- the effect of managers on the quality and standards of education and the school's ethos, not simply on management processes, structures and systems;

- the attributes and impact rather than style of leadership;

- the effectiveness of leadership and the efficiency of management as distinctive elements, taking account of the contributions of the headteacher and governors as well as other staff with management responsibilities;

- how well the school is aware of and acts on its strengths and weaknesses through its monitoring and evaluation;

- the evaluation of the headteacher and other staff;

- performance management of the school.

In SHORT INSPECTIONS, where the school is effective, evaluate why. Find out what effective leaders and efficient managers do that works.

Note: The guidance on the aspects of management, particularly performance management, will be amended as further details become available about the implementation of the 1998 Green Paper.

The guidance about how well the school is led and managed should take account of *Form S4* and must tie in with what else you have found out about the school. There is usually, but not always, a clear relationship between the standards achieved and the effectiveness of those who lead and manage. Evaluate the extent to which this causality applies.

MAKING JUDGEMENTS

Your overall judgements about how well the school is led and managed, must make sense of what else you have found out about the school, and your judgements must be consistent with those you have made elsewhere. There should be a clear relationship between the standards achieved and the effectiveness of those who lead and manage. Evaluate the extent to which those with responsibility for quality and standards in the school provide these features.

The following characteristics illustrate where to pitch judgements about how well the school is led and managed.

Very good or better	The leaders of the school share a common purpose and put pupils and their achievements first. They build co-operative and co-ordinated teams and use assessment evidence well to set high goals for pupils and challenging targets for the school and for individual staff. Staff in the school reflect critically on what they can do to improve learning and develop more effective ways of working. The work of the school is fully and thoroughly monitored, particularly the quality of teaching and its impact, and the behaviour of pupils. There is good delegation to staff with management responsibilities and effective follow-up to ensure tasks are completed well. Governors monitor performance and have a good understanding of the strengths and weaknesses of the school and the challenges it faces, and set the right priorities for development and improvement. They fulfil their statutory duties well in providing a sense of direction for the school. They understand and apply best value principles.
Satisfactory or better	The leadership and management of the school are clear about its strengths and weaknesses and have established some ways of securing improvement in the average level of standards achieved. Teamwork is mostly well established and the school has identified the right tasks for the future. Most staff share a common purpose and have taken steps to make their work more effective. Staff with particular responsibilities are clear about what these are and how they will measure their success. Governors have a sound sense of the strengths and weaknesses of the school and are working with staff in their efforts to improve. They meet their statutory responsibilities.

However, the leadership and management **are unlikely to be satisfactory** if any of these are present:

- there is a significant amount of unsatisfactory teaching;

- there is significant complacency among staff;

- standards in the school are significantly lower than they should be;

- headteacher, senior managers and governors are largely ineffective and do not know the strengths and weaknesses of the school.

Example 7.1

Successful leadership and management

One of the main reasons for the recent successes of the college is the outstanding leadership provided by its senior managers and governors, and especially by the principal. The principal brings a very clear vision of what sort of college it should be. This ensures that students achieve their best and try to do better. Teachers know their subjects and how to teach them well. Staff and students are committed to learning and have high expectations. Everything the college does seeks high quality. Governors, the vice-principal and other senior managers share this vision. The upward trend in the standards achieved by its students is just one way in which the college has been successful in fulfilling these areas.

[Excellent leadership and management (1)]

REPORTING REQUIREMENTS

SUMMARY REPORT	In both FULL and SHORT INSPECTIONS complete the table HOW WELL IS THE SCHOOL LED AND MANAGED?
	Comment on the strengths and weaknesses in leadership and management and evaluate briefly the extent to which the school applies the principles of best value.
	If any of these are features of improvement in the school report this in the section HOW THE SCHOOL HAS IMPROVED SINCE ITS LAST INSPECTION.
	If any aspects of leadership or management are particularly good or need to improve you must report under WHAT THE SCHOOL DOES WELL or WHAT COULD BE IMPROVED.
	In FULL INSPECTIONS you must include a summary judgement about the adequacy of staffing, accommodation and learning resources.
SHORT INSPECTIONS	In the commentary expand your judgements on leadership and management as reported in either WHAT THE SCHOOL DOES WELL or WHAT IT NEEDS TO IMPROVE.
FULL INSPECTIONS	Report comprehensively under the heading HOW WELL IS THE SCHOOL LED AND MANAGED?

Example 7.2

Unsuccessful leadership and management

The school's results at KS3 and at GCSE have declined steadily since 1994, when they were about in line with national averages. They are now significantly below in all subjects, a picture confirmed by the standards seen in lessons and by the quality of the teaching. The senior managers have very little knowledge of the quality of the teaching in the school. They attribute the decline in results largely to changes in the catchment area with an increase in pupils entitled to free schools meals. There is a collective sense in the staff of low expectations of the current intake of pupils, with at the same time confusion and inconsistency about standards of behaviour and how to improve them. The school has failed to understand the importance of establishing the levels of achievement of the intake year and to organise, through each subject department, accurate and consistent ways of ensuring progress is made. There has been no whole school action on the demands of reading needed for the secondary curriculum, nor does the school know whether pupils' levels of literacy enable them to read well enough for the work they have to carry out.

[Leadership and management abysmal (7)]

GUIDANCE ON USING THE CRITERIA

In all inspections the first evidence for your evaluation comes from your earliest contacts with the school. Use the school's documentation, *Forms S3* and *S4*, the previous inspection report and the *PICSI report* information to formulate some of the initial questions and hypotheses about the work and development of the school and the extent to which it promotes high standards and effective teaching and learning.

☐ **How efficiently and effectively the headteacher and key staff lead and manage the school, promoting high standards and effective teaching and learning**

Leadership is concerned with:

- creating and securing commitment to a clear vision;

- managing change so as to improve the school;

- building a high-performing team;

- inspiring, motivating and influencing staff;

- leading by example and taking responsibility.

Management is concerned with:

- strategic thinking and planning;

- people, including performance management; making best use of the skills of staff; delegation, appraisal and development;

- financial and other resources;

- communication;

- monitoring and evaluating performance and delivering results.

You will need to distinguish between leadership and management when considering the operation of the school, although the two overlap.

Do leadership and management ensure a clear direction for the work and development of the school and promote high standards?

You need to establish what is the headteacher's view of the strategic direction of the school and how far the headteacher and senior staff give a firm steer to the school's work. Apply the same perspective to the work of heads of departments and evaluate the extent to which the headteacher's leadership helps them to do a good job. Development and improvement planning should reflect the school's stated aims and objectives and promote high standards.

The evaluations that you have undertaken so far will enable you to begin to judge what aspects of standards and the success of pupils can be traced back to the impact of the school's leaders and managers. Where there are weaknesses in the work of the school and particularly in what you see in classes, you should pursue these issues with senior staff to see if they recognise them and what they have done about them.

Does the school have explicit aims and values, including a commitment to good relationships and equality of opportunity for all, which are reflected in all its work?

You will see a great deal in your first contact with the school which brings to life its stated aims and values. Evidence will come from: how the headteacher, teaching and non-teaching staff and pupils interact with each other; signs of staff and pupils being valued and the school's commitment to inclusive policies; the welcome given to visitors; the quality and care of the school environment; and pride shown in the school by staff and pupils.

In lessons, look for a sense of purpose and signs that what the school and its management stand for are reflected in teaching, for example in the approaches taken to meeting the different needs of pupils.

Talk to staff and pupils about their views of the school and what it stands for, equal opportunities, and the extent to which senior staff are interested in their work.

Is there a shared commitment to improvement and capacity to succeed?

In order to establish the school's commitment to improvements and its capacity to succeed, assess:

- whether or not standards and the expectations of teachers are high enough;

- the headteacher's skills of leadership, decision-making and communication;

- how far the headteacher and senior staff in the school know what needs to be done to improve, in what priority and how to do it;

- how aware the staff are of what needs to be done, in what order of priority, and how to do it;

- whether there is a determination by the staff to raise standards.

Does good delegation ensure the effective contribution of staff with management responsibilities?

If there are strengths or weaknesses in the work of staff responsible for co-ordination and development of subject departments, explain what these are. Consider the extent to which good delegation ensures that staff with management responsibilities contribute effectively. A good headteacher ensures that these responsibilities are clearly stated, often in job descriptions, and are effectively carried out. Look for evidence that delegation of work carries specific responsibilities and defined outcomes suited to the needs of the school, and is properly resourced.

On FULL INSPECTIONS, you should evaluate how well heads of department lead and manage their departments and their impact on the quality of teaching and the standards achieved.

In a very effective school, all staff, including support staff, know their role in its day-to-day work and longer-term improvement.

One indication of the competence and confidence of the headteacher is the way the run up to the inspection has been managed. Has the headteacher taken it in his or her stride, not allowing it to be too much of a distraction to staff and to the school's work and purpose, or has the inspection prompted unnecessary work and been allowed to induce unnecessary stress? Is on-site inspection managed well by the school?

☐ **How well the governing body fulfils its statutory responsibilities and is able to account for the performance and improvement of the school**

How well do the governors fulfil their statutory duties in helping to shape the direction of the school and do they have a good understanding of its strengths and weaknesses?

The governing body has specific statutory responsibilities, and its main tasks are: to provide a sense of direction for the work of the school; to support the work of the school as a critical friend; to hold the school to account for the standards and quality of education it achieves.

The way in which the role of the governing body or other appropriate authority is interpreted may vary significantly in relation to the school size and type, and such factors as the experience of the chair of governors and other governors. Definitions of the role of the governing body are set out in education law; the issue for you is how effectively these roles are interpreted in the context of the particular school.

In all inspections, your evaluation of the work of the governing body will need to take account of:

■ the context of the school and any impact this may have on the balance of skills, competence and commitment found in the work of governors;

■ the way the governing body ensures that the school meets with statutory requirements;

■ the relationship between the work of the headteacher and senior managers and that of the governing body;

■ the extent to which the governing body appraises the work of the headteacher and sets performance targets for the headteacher.

Your evidence will come from your discussions with the chair and other members of the governing body (including teacher governors), the headteacher and staff about:

■ the way the governors exercise their corporate role;

■ how well they fulfil their statutory duties;

■ how they help to shape the direction of the school;

■ their knowledge of the strengths and weaknesses of the school and understanding of the challenges it faces;

■ whether appropriate priorities for development and improvement are set;

■ how well they have responded to the previous inspection;

■ how governors find out for themselves how things are going;

■ whether or not they take responsibility for good and poor aspects of the school.

☐ **How effectively the school monitors and evaluates its performance, diagnoses its strengths and weaknesses, and takes effective action to secure improvement**

Is there rigorous monitoring, evaluation and development of teaching?

In all inspections you must assess how far and why the school's evaluation of teaching leads to development and improvement. Your starting points will come from *Form S4*, the last report and your judgements of standards and teaching. Look for improvement in teaching in what were the weakest subjects at the time of the last inspection and see if standards are rising. Consider:

■ the extent to which teachers are helped to analyse and draw on the approaches which work best with particular pupils;

■ how far the school knows and uses the strengths of its best teachers to influence the rest;

■ the ways in which the headteacher and other senior staff are involved in the classroom and what goes on there;

■ whether appraisal of teachers, including newly qualified teachers (NQTs), contributes to the monitoring of teaching;

■ the extent to which the headteacher's view of good and weak teaching is reflected in the work of the school;

■ how well the school helps teachers and support staff to work together;

■ whether performance targets are set for teachers.

Your evaluation must answer the following questions:

■ How well does the school monitor and analyse its standards?

■ What does it do with the information?

■ Does it face up to its weaknesses and take adequate steps to overcome them?

■ How well does it evaluate the quality of teaching?

■ What impact does all this have?

Is there effective induction of staff new to the school and is the school, or has it the potential to be, an effective provider of initial teacher training?

From September 1999 all newly qualified teachers (NQTs) must have no greater than a 90 per cent teaching load, an induction tutor and identified written targets from regular observations.

A school could be an effective provider of initial teacher training when:

■ it has professional development systems in place that are a good influence on standards of teaching;

■ it is judged to be effective overall and to have improved since its previous inspection;

■ it has a shared commitment to improvement and the capacity to succeed;

■ there is strong subject leadership and good standards of teaching.

Is there effective appraisal and performance management?

The governing body is responsible for ensuring that the headteacher is appraised and targets set, and that the school implements the national requirements for the appraisal and pay of teachers. Where you have identified important weaknesses in the performance of teachers these systems are clearly not as effective as they need to be. Evidence of effective systems for the managing teachers' performance will be seen when:

■ the deployment of resources rewards and motivates good teachers;

■ teachers work in harmony towards common goals;

■ management problems are tackled squarely;

■ capability/competency procedures are used to deal with poor performance;

■ strategies are in place to reduce staff absence;

■ appraisal and regular review assesses performance through classroom observation.

From September 1999 governing bodies have been required to operate an appraisal system for headteachers and to set targets which arise from that appraisal. You will need to evaluate their arrangements for effective appraisal.

Does the school identify appropriate priorities and targets, take the necessary action and review progress towards them?

Effective headteachers identify the right development priorities based on a clear analysis of strengths and weaknesses. In all schools you need to evaluate how far the staff know the right things to do to improve performance and whether or not they do them.

Governing bodies have to set targets for their school, that is establish specific measurable goals for improved performance by pupils. These need to be agreed with the LEA. You must evaluate how well the school uses assessment and performance data to predict potential, focus effort and support improvement. Schools vary greatly in character and each finds its own particular way to raise achievement. This process is likely to be most effective if it involves all staff. Where a school knows how good its standards are and how good its teaching is, it is well placed to set targets for itself, take the necessary action and review progress towards them.

Much of your evidence of the effectiveness of target setting will be derived from your evaluation of how high standards are and whether they are high enough. Examine in particular the extent to which:

- the school makes good use of data on pupils' attainment on entry;

- information from standardised tests is used effectively;

- the school questions itself about the performance of different individuals and groups of pupils, and reviews its own performance against that for other schools, and present as against past performance;

- the school's priorities and targets are appropriate and linked with clear programmes of action;

- procedures are in place to monitor the outcomes of this work.

☐ **The extent to which the school makes best strategic use of its resources, including specific grants and additional funding, linking decisions on spending to educational priorities**

How well are educational priorities supported through careful financial management and planning?

An efficient school demonstrates that it budgets systematically for all expenditure and is clear about the cost of its development. Your emphasis should not be on the detail of the financial planning, but rather on the extent to which the school's spending decisions relate to priorities for improvement and to benefit for pupils. Once priorities have been identified you will need to find out the extent to which the school has applied the best value principles of competition in, for example, obtaining tenders for services or goods (*see Annex 1*).

Your overriding judgement on the use made by the school of its financial resources and newly developed technologies will be on how far all pupils benefit from wisely targeted spending. Much of the evidence you require for this judgement will be found in lessons.

If you need to investigate further, detailed school information will be found in *Form S2* and must be supplemented by discussion with appropriate staff in the school, particularly the finance officer, where this is not the headteacher. Your evaluation will concentrate on the logic and quality of links between planning and spending.

Another feature of careful financial planning is effective financial control and administration. You are not conducting a detailed financial audit but you must have access to the latest auditors' report. Establish whether:

- the main recommendations in the report have been acted upon;

- systems for financial administration are unobtrusive, efficient and responsive to need;

- financial administration keeps the way clear for teachers to concentrate on their work;

- adequate information is available to the headteacher and governors to ensure that finances are kept in good order and costs easily determined.

In 11–18 schools, you should analyse the post-16 funding and expenditure. Schools can deploy their resources between the main school and post-16 as they see fit, but unless there are good strategic reasons for an imbalance, you should expect to see the proportion of expenditure on post-16 provision to be roughly the same as the proportion of the budget generated by the registration of post-16 students. Inspection contractors have a disk which will help you with this analysis.

The post-16 curriculum may include joint provision with other schools and/or with Further Education Funding Council (FEFC) sector colleges. Alternatively, franchising or purchasing arrangements may be used to provide vocational or minority A/AS level courses. Strategies used by some schools for reducing the costs of small groups include combining AS and A level classes, combining year groups and using supported self-study with reduced teacher contact time. There are further details in the *Inspecting Subjects and Aspects 11–18* booklet about sixth forms.

Example 7.3

Extract from an inspection report of a secondary school

The school progressively adds value during both Key Stage 3 and Key Stage 4. Pupils' attainments overall are well above average by the time they reach the age of 16. Their achievements are good. The deployment of staff makes effective use of their expertise and most of the teaching is good or very good. Accommodation has areas of high quality and parts that need improving. Resources used in the classrooms are generally a little above average and are used well. Pupils' attainments on entry to the school are above average. These factors, considered in relation to a cost per pupil which is higher than average, indicate a very good school which is providing satisfactory value for money.

[Overall: a very good school (2) giving satisfactory value for money 4)]

Is effective use made of new technologies, including ICT?

During the inspection ask about the use the school is making of new technologies, including ICT, electronic mail, multi-media compositions, data analysis, CD-ROM, the National Grid for Learning, and Internet applications. Evaluate the role of senior staff in ensuring the effective use of this technology.

Are specific grants used effectively for their designated purpose?

Where a school is in receipt of a specific grant, for instance the Ethnic Minorities Achievement Grant (EMAG), evaluate how well the school is using this money for its designated purpose. Make sure the additional funds are used for their intended purposes by considering:

■ the extent to which the funds are appropriately allocated;

■ how well the school monitors the effectiveness of the spending;

■ whether the outcomes of the expenditure match the objectives;

■ how well the school uses additional grants related to the school's provision, for example for teaching, curriculum and advertisement.

☐ The extent to which the principles of best value are applied in the school's use of resources

To what extent are best value principles of comparison, challenge, consultation and competition applied in the school's management and use of resources?

Detailed guidance on the concepts embodied in best value principles can be found in Annex 1 of this *Handbook*. In all inspections the use the school makes of best value principles must be evaluated.

Schools applying best value principles will recognise the importance of questions such as:

- How do our standards and costs **compare** with those of other schools?

- How do we **challenge** ourselves to justify the use of resources to provide educational activities outside the statutory curriculum, for instance parent–school partnerships and vocational courses?

- How do we satisfy ourselves that **competition** is fair where we buy contracted-out services, for instance school meals?

- How widely do we **consult**, for example on major spending decisions and changes to the curriculum?

The answers to these questions will tell you how well the school is applying the best value principles.

☐ The adequacy of staffing, accommodation and learning resources, highlighting strengths and weaknesses in different subjects and areas of the curriculum where they affect the quality of education provided and the educational standards achieved

Do the number, qualifications and experience of teachers and support staff match the demands of the curriculum?

In FULL INSPECTIONS only, evaluate the extent to which the school is staffed and resourced to teach the curriculum and whether there are any features that contribute to or detract from good quality and high standards. A good school makes the best use of all its available resources to achieve the highest possible standards for all its pupils.

Evaluate how far the staff are qualified to teach the school's curriculum, including post-16 subjects and courses, are trained or experienced in the appropriate phase and the extent to which levels of staffing ensure that all pupils are taught effectively. Consider whether there are enough skilled support staff to enable the school to function effectively. Take into account the qualifications and experience of those staff in relation to the needs of the pupils in the school. You should give particular attention to the effectiveness of the use of staff working with pupils who have special education needs and with those for whom English is an additional language.

When considering the adequacy of the **number, qualifications and experience of teachers and support staff** keep in mind that:

- in many schools, other staff provide complementary support for the work of teachers;

- in an effective team all staff understand their role as well as those of others;

- staff should be trained and experienced to provide the appropriate age-related curriculum;

- every school should have a co-ordinator for special educational needs;

■ additional support may be provided for some pupils with statements of special educational needs and for those for whom English is an additional language;

■ a school that is a designated support base or unit for pupils with statements will have prescribed staffing levels.

Where the school is affected by staff illness or a pattern of absence comes to your attention, you should evaluate what the school does to support staff and reduce staff absence.

Does the accommodation allow the curriculum to be taught effectively? Are learning resources adequate for the school's curriculum and range of pupils?

Your evaluation of the adequacy and effectiveness of accommodation and learning resources should be informed by particular strengths and weaknesses identified during the inspection, noting where provision enhances or detracts from pupils learning well in different subjects. Evaluate the quality of the accommodation, including outdoor areas, particularly for the younger pupils, and whether they provide a stimulating and well-maintained place for pupils to learn and play. Judge the adequacy and effectiveness of learning resources according to the level of provision, its appropriateness, condition and accessibility. You should judge the effectiveness of the library by the ways in which it promotes higher levels of literacy for all pupils in the full range of the curriculum; by its support for effective and challenging teaching; by the way it is a multi-media resource for personal study; by its contribution in enabling and encouraging pupils to read widely and confidently; and the extent to which pupils value reading as a source of pleasure and information. Make your judgements and record your evidence about accommodation and resources **only where provision has a significant impact on standards.**

8. WHAT SHOULD THE SCHOOL DO TO IMPROVE FURTHER?

The report must include:

☐ specific matters – key issues – which the appropriate authority for the school should include in its post-inspection action plan, listed as issues for action in order of their importance in raising standards in the school;

Each issue must be followed by a reference to the main paragraph(s) in the inspection report where the weaknesses are discussed.

These issues should be based on any weaknesses identified in the inspection and include all the matters listed in WHAT COULD BE IMPROVED in relation to **standards** achieved and the **quality of education** provided, with particular emphasis on **teaching**.

Where the inspection highlights issues already identified as priorities in the school's development plan, this section should acknowledge this.

Any non-compliance with statutory requirements where it detracts significantly from the quality and standards of the school or where it relates to care, health and safety should be reported here.

☐ a statement indicating paragraphs of the inspection report which refer to other weaknesses, not included in issues for action, but which should be considered by the school.

INSPECTION FOCUS

This section of the report is linked directly to the statements made in the summary under the heading WHAT COULD BE IMPROVED. In that section, you need to summarise the school's main weaknesses, without, at that stage, giving the direction in which the school might move to bring about improvements. The statements included in WHAT SHOULD THE SCHOOL DO TO IMPROVE FURTHER? take that step. They set out what needs to be done to bring about improvement. You must not go further than this to indicate how the school could take the required action; that is the proper remit of the school's governors and staff. You must make it absolutely clear what needs to be done, breaking down the statement into several parts if it helps to clarify what the school must do.

☐ **Specific matters – key issues – which the appropriate authority for the school should include in its post-inspection action plan, listed as issues for action in order of their importance in raising standards in the school**

Each bullet point in the section WHAT COULD BE IMPROVED must, one by one, be covered in this section so that the reader can immediately link each issue for action by the school to an inspection judgement. You must use this section to make it very clear to the school the steps they must take to bring about the improvement that you have identified. This means that you will almost certainly need to use a list format with a number of actions under a heading linked back to the bullet point in WHAT COULD BE IMPROVED.

These key issues should be the big issues for the school, and not matters which are less significant. The detail of this section must naturally lead the school to improvement. A compliance issue should only be included here if it detracts significantly from the quality of the school's provision or the standards that pupils can attain. In a SHORT INSPECTION, the effectiveness of the school means that it is unlikely that there will be significant compliance issues, but if they do arise they should be indicated here. In a FULL INSPECTION, you should avoid making a long list of compliance issues here unless they are significant.

☐ **A statement indicating paragraphs of the report which refer to other weaknesses not included in issues for action, but which should be considered by the school**

In FULL INSPECTIONS only, you should use this statement to bring to the attention of the school those weaknesses which need to be considered by the school but which do not appear as one of the main areas for improvement. You should also use this statement to include compliance issues which, although important, do not significantly detract from the education pupils receive or the standards they achieve.

9. OTHER SPECIFIED FEATURES

Where additional features are specified for inspection, inspectors must evaluate and report on:

☐ the overall effectiveness of each feature.

In determining their judgements, inspectors should consider the extent to which:

• one or more specified criteria are met.

SCHOOL DATA AND INDICATORS

PART C OF THE INSPECTION REPORT

After OTHER SPECIFIED FEATURES, if any, the inspection report will contain data and indicators which are defined by the report template which is in use at the time of the inspection.

THE INSPECTION OF OTHER FEATURES

The inspection focus for any additional features for inspection, for example a survey of an issue in secondary schools over a particular term, will be specified along with the feature itself.

Each feature specified will be accompanied by:

- an evaluation and reporting requirement indicated by □;

- up to three inspection criteria;

- a commentary covering the inspection focus;

- a summary of reporting requirements;

- guidance in the format of this *Handbook*, including sections on the inspection focus, making your judgement, and guidance on the inspection criteria.

10. THE STANDARDS AND QUALITY OF TEACHING IN AREAS OF THE CURRICULUM, SUBJECTS AND COURSES

FULL INSPECTIONS ONLY – PART D OF THE INSPECTION REPORT

Subjects and courses

For each subject or course, where evidence allows, the report should include evaluation of:

☐ standards of work in the subject, and how well pupils achieve, particularly the standards achieved by the oldest pupils in each Key Stage, highlighting what pupils do well and could do better;

☐ changes since the previous inspection;

☐ how well pupils are taught, highlighting effective and ineffective teaching in the subjects and relating the demands made by teachers to pupils' learning and the progress they have made;

☐ any other factors which have a bearing on what is achieved, especially the extent to which management of this subject is directed towards monitoring, evaluating and improving performance.

In English and mathematics, the subject reports of pupils' work up to 16 should draw on evidence of the contribution made by other subjects to pupils' competence in literacy, particularly reading, writing and numeracy respectively. In information and communications technology (ICT), the report should draw on evidence of contributions made to pupils' IT capability from all other subjects.

In schools with pupils of secondary age, the report should include sections on all subjects of the curriculum up to and post-16, and any other courses or subjects included in the inspection contract. In secondary schools with post-16 provision, the section should provide reports on vocational courses and other post-16 provision. *Inspecting Subjects and Aspects 11–18* provides detailed further guidance. GNVQ or other vocational courses can be grouped together unless the inspection contract includes the inspection of specific component courses.

PART 2

GUIDANCE FOR INSPECTORS ON CONDUCTING INSPECTIONS AND WRITING REPORTS

INSPECTION QUALITY

1. This guidance will help you to interpret the inspection requirements set out in *Inspecting Schools*, the inspection Framework. It follows the sequence of work required before, during and after an inspection.

2. The guidance is for all inspectors and contractors. The registered inspector is ultimately responsible for the inspection and the report. This guidance therefore focuses particularly on his/her role. However, all inspectors in a team must work to the inspection requirements set out here, especially the Code of Conduct, and measure up to the Quality Guarantee for teachers. The inspection contractor has to meet OFSTED's Quality Assurance Standard as a condition for being awarded inspection work.

Setting a standard for inspection

3. As an inspector, you need to have high personal and professional qualities. When inspecting, you should treat all the people you meet – pupils, parents, staff, governors and others – as you would expect them to treat you, with interest, courtesy and respect. You should regard your right of entry to schools as a privilege.

4. Assessing the professional competence of others can arouse anxieties. Inspection is no exception. You must see to it that you recognise and praise strengths as well as probe areas of weakness. You must be alert to the sensitivities of staff but also be objective in all you do.

5. There are four main strands to inspection:

   - finding out what the school is like, and its strengths and weaknesses;

   - diagnosing what makes it the way it is;

   - identifying what it needs to do next to improve;

   - reflecting these findings back to the school, both orally and in the written inspection report.

6. Inspection is effective when it is seen by schools as fair, rigorous and helpful. The school must respect and value the quality and expertise of the inspection team. If it does, it will accept and make use of the inspection's findings to help it move forward. Otherwise, the usefulness of inspection is greatly reduced.

7. Inspection, therefore, must not only arrive at the right judgements but also be done in the right way.

Quality Guarantee for schools

8   We attach such a high priority to the effect of inspection on schools, that we expect all inspectors actively to reflect and promote the Quality Guarantee we give to teachers.

QUALITY GUARANTEE

- *Inspectors will do everything possible to work with you in keeping the stress of an inspection to a minimum.*

- *Inspectors will not expect you to create additional paperwork specifically for the inspection.*

- *Inspectors will always treat you in a courteous and friendly manner, particularly when entering and leaving your classroom.*

- *Normally, you will be observed teaching for no more than half of any one day, and never more than three-quarters.*

- *Inspectors will not judge teaching unless they have observed a significant part of the lesson, normally for at least 30 minutes.*

- *Inspectors will use confidential information responsibly.*

- *Inspectors will discuss important aspects of your teaching with you.*

- *Inspectors will explain the reasons for their judgements and be helpful in identifying where improvement is needed.*

---

9   Most inspectors reflect these principles naturally in their work. The great majority of the responses we receive from teachers and schools show that most inspectors have high standards of conduct and professionalism.

10   But there are exceptions. There is no place for inspectors who are remote from the teachers, brusque, overbearing in their behaviour, or insensitive. Nor should you ask the school for paperwork it does not normally use, such as lesson plans to a particular format.

OFSTED's expectations of inspectors

11   Our expectations of inspectors are set out in the Framework and include the following.

12   **You must be thoroughly prepared for the inspection and understand the context of the school and its pupils.** It takes time to prepare properly. You should ensure that the contractor gives you enough time. If you are a registered inspector, the quality of your *Pre-Inspection Commentary* is vital. If the issues it identifies are clear, and you brief your team well, the inspection will get off to a good start.

13   **You must have thorough knowledge and understanding of the Framework, this *Inspection Handbook*, the subjects and aspects you inspect and the age range of the pupils concerned.** You work in a changing educational scene. Curriculum requirements change, as do the national policies. You must keep yourself up to date. This means consulting documents from various sources: from OFSTED, the DfEE, the Qualifications and Curriculum Authority and other relevant bodies. You need to be aware of the different kinds of provision in Key Stage 4, for example the

work-related curriculum. Equally, members of the team must be conversant with provision for students post-16.

14   You must uphold the highest professional standards required by the Code of Conduct, thus securing OFSTED's Quality Guarantee to teachers *(see above)*.

CODE OF CONDUCT

15   The Code of Conduct has been revised. To meet its principles, you must:

■ **evaluate the work of the school objectively, be impartial and have no previous connection with the school, its staff or governors which could undermine your objectivity;**

> We take the questions of impartiality and connection seriously. If you have had anything to do with the school in the past few years, you should consider carefully whether you should be part of the school's inspection team. You should certainly rule yourself out if this contact included any 'pre-inspection' work, staff appointments, advice or staff development. If in doubt, you should err on the side of caution. If you are a team inspector you must, as a condition of your enrolment, inform the registered inspector and contractor of any connection at all with the school.

■ **report honestly and fairly, ensuring that judgements accurately and reliably reflect what the school achieves and does;**

> Judgements must be robust and fully supported by evidence so that you can defend them, if required. They must be accurate and carefully weighed and tested against the inspection criteria. They must also be reliable, which means that other trained inspectors, using the same evidence, would be highly likely to come to the same judgement.

■ **carry out your work with integrity, treating all those you meet with courtesy and sensitivity;**

> It is important that you leave staff feeling as though they have been treated well and fairly.

■ **do all you can to minimise stress, in particular by ensuring that no teacher is over-inspected and by not asking for paperwork to be specifically prepared for the inspection;**

> We are committed to reducing stress among teachers as far as possible. Inspectors must do everything they can to allay anxiety. This must start from the moment they begin to have dealings with the school and continue until the report is published. Teachers are naturally apprehensive about inspection. We expect you to do what you can to put them at their ease. There are clear guidelines about how much teachers should be observed during a day. In secondary schools, all inspectors share the responsibility to ensure that these guidelines are followed.

■ **act with the best interests and well-being of pupils and staff as priorities;**

> The deal the pupils get is at the heart of your work. It is essential that you discover their views of the school as well as evaluating their educational progress and achievements. You must certainly not cause pupils any anxiety. You have many dealings with them during an inspection. Your questioning should not make them feel vulnerable or inadequate. Your relations with them must be a model of propriety. You must not put them in a position where they may feel conflicting loyalties.

■ **communicate with staff purposefully and productively, and present your judgements of the school's work clearly and frankly;**

> In your dealings with teachers, you should build confidence and mutual respect. You should seek to understand what they are doing and why, and share with them your views about what you find. We cannot stress enough the importance of feeding back your findings in a helpful way.

■ **respect the confidentiality of information, particularly about teachers and the judgements made about their individual teaching.**

> In judging teaching, you are undertaking a form of professional appraisal. You should not criticise the work of a teacher, or anyone else involved with the school, within earshot of someone else. You should relay concerns to the headteacher or appropriate manager, but not before discussing them with the teacher concerned. Do not allow yourself to be placed in a position where you cannot use information you are given in the way you think best. At times, you may need to make it clear that you reserve the right to do as you see fit with certain information or evidence.

THE RECORD OF INSPECTION EVIDENCE

16   The record of evidence comprises:

i.   forms completed by the school:

- *Form S1* – consultation with the appropriate authority about the specification for the inspection, and data about the school;

- *Form S2* – further data about the school;

- *Form S3* – school self-audit;

- *Form S4* – school monitoring and self-evaluation;

ii.   the *PICSI report* supplied by OFSTED;

iii.   documentary evidence from the school (normally returned to the school after the inspection) and the previous inspection report;

iv.   evidence and judgements recorded by inspectors, including:

- *Pre-Inspection Commentary*, with issues for inspection;

- *Evidence Forms*;

- *Inspection Notebooks* – one is completed by each member of the team on FULL INSPECTIONS (optional in SHORT INSPECTIONS);

- the *Record of Corporate Judgements*;

- evidence from parents.

17   Further details of the record of evidence are given in the sections which follow. Instructions for their completion are summarised in Annex 3.

EFFICIENT AND EFFECTIVE INSPECTION

18   The process of inspection, like developing a photographic image, is the progressive unveiling of the school until its essential character can be seen. As each part of the picture is revealed the image becomes clearer. Because inspection is such a concentrated process, from the start it must use all the evidence available to hypothesise about the school's quality and standards, and its potential strengths and weaknesses. This gives a focus for the inspectors' work.

19   However, inspection is not a mere snapshot of a school. The quality and standards of each school in England are now documented in one or more previous inspection reports. Each school's performance has been measured, year after year. The school's own planning also reflects its changing priorities and needs. Each school has an ongoing record, showing where it has come from: a performance trail.

THE INSPECTION SEQUENCE

20   The registered inspector should take full account of the recent history of the school's quality and standards, particularly when gauging the extent of improvement. Much of the information needed is presented in the *Pre-Inspection Context and School Indicator (PICSI) report*. Most schools have detailed performance data to augment the *PICSI* indicators.

21   You should also note what the school does to monitor and evaluate its own performance and what its evaluation shows. The inspection forms the school completes reflect the wish of many schools for inspectors to take self-evaluation into account.[1] *Form S3* invites the school to make its own assessment of compliance with statutory requirements: a self-audit. *Form S4* invites the school to present its own view of where it stands in relation to each of the areas of its work to be inspected. Using inspection to test the school's perceptions of itself gives an insight into how well it is managed. Inspection thus provides a mirror for the school.

22   The first stage of pre-inspection analysis should provide early hypotheses to follow up at the preliminary visit to the school. This visit should give you, as the registered inspector, a very helpful first impression of the *quality* of the school. It may be difficult for some headteachers to be available for discussion during the school day. By meeting the headteacher, staff, governors and pupils, and by looking round the school, you will get an important contextual picture to set alongside the data and documentary evidence.

23   You should now be in a position to complete most of the *Pre-Inspection Commentary* for the rest of the inspection team. Ideally this should take into account the views of parents, although this may depend on the timing of the parents' meeting. Your analysis must identify important issues and lines of enquiry for the inspection. Some of these may relate to apparent areas of strength or weakness, others to:

■ issues for action identified in the last inspection;

■ claims made by the school in its self-evaluation report;

---

[1]   This was also recommended by the Education and Employment Committee of the House of Commons, Fourth Report, *The Work of OFSTED*, London 1999.

■ features that relate to the school's particular circumstances;

■ areas identified by the headteacher for inspection.

Above all, the issues must be specific to the school.

24   The *Pre-Inspection Commentary* has three purposes. First, it forms the basis for briefing other members of the team so that they know a great deal about the school when they arrive to start the inspection. Secondly, it provides an agenda of inspection priorities. Thirdly, it contributes to the judgements for the inspection report.

25   As the inspection progresses, there is often a change in emphasis, from establishing what the standards are and how well they reflect the earlier data, to securing explanations of why the achievements of the school are as they are. The quality of teaching will be an early focus.

26   At the end of the inspection, there should be a clear and shared view among the whole inspection team of the overall quality and standards of the school. In other words, how good it is. You should evaluate against each of the main requirements of the inspection schedule, and the team should reach a consensus view on the school's strengths, any areas for improvement, and what the school needs to do to improve. This process is summarised below.

The inspection sequence

Before the inspection	During the inspection	At the end of the inspection

Pre-inspection analysis provides an initial view of the standards and possible quality of the school, influenced by visiting the school and hearing the views of the parents.

Initial emphasis on verifying the standards of the school and evaluating the quality of its provision. As the inspection proceeds, the relative impact of different factors is assessed.

Inspectors agree their judgements about standards, quality, strengths and weaknesses, focusing on teaching, leadership and management.

Finally they identify what the school should do to improve.

BEFORE THE INSPECTION

NOTICE OF INSPECTION

27   OFSTED has reduced the notice of inspection given to schools to between six and ten school weeks. The purpose of this is to reduce the pressure on teachers and other staff, and to avoid long, drawn-out processes, such as rewriting documents and making other preparations which some schools have felt they needed to do. The shorter notice has been welcomed by most schools. However, it does put some pressure on the school to complete the inspection forms on time, and on the contractor and registered inspector to make the necessary arrangements for the inspection.

28   The shorter notice of inspection places a premium on efficient procedures in the run-up to inspection. The inspection will take place during a five-week 'inspection window'. The possible sequence of pre-inspection events is illustrated below. The first five steps are fixed by the 'inspection window'; the others will vary slightly in timing, depending on the date of the inspection.

Summary of pre-inspection steps

Six school weeks before the 'inspection window' (typically eight weeks before the inspection)	1. School receives notification of inspection, and whether this will be SHORT or FULL, a set of inspection forms, and a copy of the *PICSI report*	
Five school weeks before the inspection window (typically seven weeks before the inspection)	2. School returns *Form S1* to OFSTED	3. Contractor receives specification and *PICSI report* from OFSTED with *Form S1* and sets date of inspection with school and registered inspector 4. Registered inspector contacts school
Two school weeks before the inspection window (typically four weeks before the inspection)		5. Contractor sends outline inspection plan to OFSTED and item list to OFSTED and the school
Four weeks before the inspection	6. School sends *Forms S2–S4*, plus previous inspection report, prospectus and development plan to registered inspector and calls meeting for parents	7. Registered inspector receives documents from school, and prepares for visit
Two or three weeks before the inspection		8. Registered inspector visits school 9. Registered inspector plans the inspection in detail
Two weeks before the inspection		10. Registered inspector meets parents 11. Registered inspector completes *Pre-Inspection Commentary*
Before the inspection begins		12. Registered inspector meets and briefs team

STEPS 1 AND 2: INSPECTION SPECIFICATION

29   As soon as the school is notified of the inspection and whether it is to be SHORT or FULL, it is asked to complete *Form S1* and return it to OFSTED within a week. At the same time, OFSTED supplies the school with *Forms S2, S3* and *S4*, which the school has three weeks to complete in electronic or hardcopy format.

30   *Form S1* allows the appropriate authority to provide basic information about the nature and composition of the school. *Form S1* is used to draw up the specification which OFSTED issues to the contractor as part of the contract for inspection; it will help the contractor to determine the composition of the inspection team.

STEP 3: SETTING THE DATE

31   Once it has the specification, the contractor should move immediately to let the school know who is to be the registered inspector, and to establish the date of the inspection with the school and the registered inspector.

STEP 4: COMMUNICATING WITH THE SCHOOL AND PARENTS

32   If you are the registered inspector for the inspection, you should make contact with the headteacher of the school and:

- introduce yourself;

- find out how the headteacher, staff and governors are viewing the forthcoming inspection;

- enquire about progress in completing the *Forms S2–S4* and arrange for them to be *sent to you*, together with the other prescribed documents (*see paragraph 34*);

- arrange a date and time to visit the school, explaining what you wish to do during the visit, and set up a programme for it;

- discuss and agree dates and times for other events, including the parents' meeting, feedback to senior management team and governing body or appropriate authority, the period over which the school can check the draft report, and the days the inspection will last;

- check that the school has received the *PICSI report* from OFSTED;

- make the CVs of the inspection team available to the school.

STEPS 5, 6 AND 7: INITIAL PREPARATION

33   To make the most of your visit to the school you must prepare thoroughly. Contractors must make sure that time is provided for this.

34   You first need to assemble the core documents required before the visit. These are:

- *Form S1*, completed by the school and sent to you by OFSTED;

- *Forms S2, S3* and *S4* completed and sent to you by the school;

- the *PICSI report*, provided by OFSTED;

- the last inspection report, provided by the school;

- the current school development or management plan, provided by the school;

- the school prospectus or brochure, provided by the school.

35   You must not require any other documents from the school at this stage. The school has enough to do in completing the four forms, calling the parents' meeting and communicating with governors. Remember that the inspection must do everything possible to avoid putting an extra burden on schools or significantly affecting their normal patterns of work.

36   Your analysis of indicators and documents should be systematic and your enquiries related to the questions posed in the inspection *Schedule*. WHAT SORT OF SCHOOL IS IT? is both the starting and the finishing point for your inspection. Start with the school's view of itself, expressed in its prospectus. Look at how it presents itself and what it considers to be important. Consider the extent to which pupils' interests are at the centre of the school's presentation and aspirations.

37   *Forms S1* and *S2* indicate who the pupils are, their background, mobility, home language and special educational needs. Look for evidence of effectiveness. Look at the pattern of the school's results, trends over time, high and low spots, and comparative data. Look at other indications of effectiveness, such as how the budget is constructed; the pattern of exclusions, if there are any; and attendance.

38   Then your analysis can move from outcomes to the quality of provision. Look at the curriculum as expressed qualitatively in the prospectus and quantitatively on *Form S2*. Consider whether it is giving the range of experiences you might expect, across the age range. Consider staffing and class organisation, the staff profile and deployment, and possible management issues. Look for the school's priorities for improvement reflected in the development plan.

39   After this analysis you should have a useful but partial picture of the school. This will include hypotheses that you will need to investigate further. What does this picture add up to? Where has the school come from and where is it heading? What appear to be the big issues in the school? What are the school's targets and is it likely to meet them? Three strong pieces of evidence are: the previous inspection report; the headteacher's evaluation report on *Form S4*; and the *PICSI* report.

40   By putting the information from these different sources together, you should be able to: estimate how the school is performing; know what its priorities now are; see whether these have changed since the last inspection; and consider how the school views its own quality and standards. You will have an initial impression of the school which will form the basis for discussion when you meet the headteacher.

41   You are now in a position to begin to write the *Pre-Inspection Commentary*, which you will add to significantly and complete after the preliminary visit to the school. You should include views about:

- standards attained in the core subjects of English, mathematics and science, highlighting any patterns of strengths or weaknesses;

- trends in attainment over time, where appropriate;

- whether or not, according to quantitative indicators, the school has improved since its last inspection;

- areas that might need further exploration during the inspection;

- the quality of management.

STEP 8: VISITING THE SCHOOL

42   The visit to the school is a very important part of the inspection process and is likely to last for a day. It has five main purposes:

i.   to establish a good and trusting working relationship between you (the registered inspector) and the school, particularly the headteacher;

ii.   to gain a better understanding of the school, its nature, what it is aiming to do and how it goes about its work;

iii.   to consider aspects of the school on which inspectors might focus, some of which may be identified by the school;

iv.   to brief the staff and any governors who are able to meet you on how the inspection will work;

v.   to agree the necessary arrangements for the inspection.

43   To achieve these intentions you will need to plan the visit carefully, in consultation with the headteacher.

44   Ideally, you will need to do the following during the initial visit:

- have an extensive discussion with the headteacher to find out more about the school and the way it is run, and to test your initial perceptions; and tour the school, to become acquainted with its geography, if possible meeting some pupils and staff;

- meet the staff of the school, to brief them on how the inspection will be organised and respond to any queries they may have;

- meet any representatives of the governing body, again to discuss the inspection with them, but also to learn how the governing body has been involved with developments since the last inspection, and how it perceives its current role and priorities. You should arrange to meet governors during the inspection as well.

45 Your meetings with the headteacher, staff and governors should put them at their ease by explaining how the inspection will be run, and give them confidence in the process. They should be helped to see how they can gain value from it. You should explain:

For a SHORT INSPECTION

■ how the SHORT INSPECTION can only be a light 'health check' of the school, not an intensive subject-by-subject inspection;

■ the basis for sampling lessons, with the possibility that some teachers or subjects will not be seen;

■ that inspectors will discuss work with teachers as they go, giving whatever feedback they can;

■ that the report will focus on the main strengths of the school and areas needing improvement.

For a FULL INSPECTION

■ that a significant amount of the work in every subject will be seen, though individual teachers may be observed on only one or two occasions;

■ how all teachers will be offered feedback on their work and receive their profile of lesson grades.

46 Discuss with the headteacher the arrangements for the parents' meeting. Discuss whether the school can provide a room for the inspection team to work in during the inspection. If the school is unable to do this without disturbing its own work, the inspectors will have to make their own arrangements for a base.

47 During the preliminary visit, you should request from the school any additional documents which will be needed in advance of the inspection. These must be those which the school already has, or can easily supply. You should not ask the headteacher to prepare additional documents specifically for the inspection. To make the inspection run smoothly, you will need:

■ a programme, or timetable, of the school's work in the period of the inspection;

■ a staff handbook, if one is available, or list of staff responsibilities and/or objectives;

■ a plan of the school.

48 In a FULL INSPECTION, you will need to take away, or see at a later stage, further documents such as:

■ the governors' annual report to parents;

■ minutes of the meetings of the governing body, or the equivalent where the 'appropriate authority' is not the governing body;

■ evidence of progress towards the targets set by governors;

■ curriculum plans, policies, guidelines or schemes of work already in existence;

■ the outcomes of self-evaluations carried out recently by the school;

■ the outcomes of any external monitoring and evaluations carried out since the last inspection;

■ a copy of the most recent audit report;

■ any other documentation the school wishes you to consider, subject to your agreement.

You should return all of these to the school after the inspection.

49 In a SHORT INSPECTION, you should avoid taking further documentation away from the school. You should not ask the school to collect together curriculum plans, policies, guidelines or schemes of work, no matter how important the school feels they are. Only if specific issues arise during the inspection, where the reasons for a particular strength or weakness need be explored, should you ask to see any related material.

50 There is a lot of ground to cover on the preliminary visit; therefore it is not ideal to hold the parents' meeting on the same day.

STEP 9: PLANNING THE INSPECTION

51 The registered inspector should:

- ensure responsibilities are assigned for all subjects and aspects, special educational needs, equal opportunities; and, where relevant, the sixth form and English as an additional language;

- decide the deployment of the team on the basis of a clear strategy for sampling the work of the school, taking account of the areas of expertise of team members;

- plan the deployment of inspectors, particularly on the first day, and ensure that each inspector has an appropriate schedule of inspection activities to cover in addition to his/her responsibilities;

- plan to collect evidence relating to particular aspects identified as focal points in the *Pre-Inspection Commentary*;

- plan, in conjunction with the school, when discussions with staff will take place and, on FULL INSPECTIONS, agree when the feedback to subject co-ordinators and classroom teachers will be held;

- in SHORT INSPECTIONS, decide whether or not *Inspection Notebooks* will be used;

- set deadlines for team inspectors to complete *Inspection Notebooks* (remember that, apart from the draft sections for the report, these must be completed before the final team meeting);

- in FULL INSPECTIONS, set deadlines for team inspectors to submit draft sections for the report.

STEP 10: MEETING WITH PARENTS

52 The pre-inspection meeting with parents is a legal requirement. The meeting must take place before the inspection begins so that the registered inspector can fully consider the parents' views as important pre-inspection evidence. Parents should have as much notice of the meeting as possible. The 'appropriate authority' (usually the governing body) is responsible for organising the meeting. Only parents of pupils registered at the school should be invited. The headteacher or one of the governors, usually the chair, may introduce you to the parents at the meeting. Any member of staff, or governor, who is also a parent of a pupil at the school may attend the meeting. OFSTED provides a sample letter of invitation and the suggested agenda for the meeting (available on the CD-ROM attached to this *Handbook*).

53 The registered inspector should invite the governing body to distribute the standard questionnaire to parents (available on the CD-ROM). Individual responses are confidential to the inspection team and there should be arrangements to ensure that this is the case. Inspection contractors have translations of the questionnaire in the more commonly used home languages and at an early stage you should check with the school whether these are needed. If forms in other languages are used, you will need to plan to have comments translated.

54 The school should distribute the questionnaire on the basis of one per pupil. However, its normal procedures should be used where information is sent separately to more than one person with responsibility for the child, making sure that sufficient questionnaires are sent so that parents can respond separately for each child.

55 You should base the meeting on the standard agenda for parents' meetings (available on the CD-ROM) and give parents the opportunity to express their views on:

- the standards the school achieves;

- how the school helps pupils, whatever their ability, to learn and make progress;

- the attitudes and values the school promotes;

- behaviour and attendance;

- the work the school expects pupils to do at home; and the school's links with parents, including information on how pupils are getting on;

- how the school responds to parents' suggestions and concerns;

- how the school has improved in recent years.

56 You should also invite views on any other matters which the parents may wish to raise. You should ask parents not to name individual pupils and teachers at any stage during the meeting. You should explain in general terms the forthcoming inspection and its purpose. You may need to explain why the school has been selected for a particular type of inspection.

57 As soon as possible after the meeting is over, and you have received the returned questionnaires and analysed them, you should discuss with the headteacher the significant issues and concerns raised by parents. You should give the headteacher the opportunity to offer you other evidence of parents' views about the school. You should explain that the inspectors' views on what parents say about the school will form part of the feedback at the end of the inspection, and also will be contained in the written report.

STEP 11: COMPLETION OF THE *PRE-INSPECTION COMMENTARY*

58 After the visit to the school, you should be in a position to prepare a detailed, well-informed and penetrating *Pre-Inspection Commentary* on the school. This commentary should be completed for as many sections of the schedule as possible.

59 You should give preliminary views about:

- the characteristics of the school;

- standards, trends in attainment, and improvement since the last inspection, adding to your existing commentary on these areas;

- attendance and exclusions, with potential views on attitudes and behaviour;

- the match of staff expertise to subjects taught and any implications for attainment shown in the data;

- the range and quality of the school's educational provision and other aspects of the school, making full use of the school's documents provided.

60 You should present initial hypotheses about why the standards achieved are as they are and any significant variation over time and between subjects or groups of pupils. You should highlight in particular those features of the school that appear to impact on standards, such as:

- possible changes in the quality of teaching caused by staff turnover, monitoring and evaluation strategies, or in-service training;

- features of the school's context and organisation such as mixed-aged classes;

- the impact of the school's context and its leadership and management;

- changes in curriculum provision, such as the introduction of the National Literacy and Numeracy strategies;

- the use of resources to promote standards.

61 These are matters that you must pursue in the inspection. You should also form hypotheses about:

- the extent, and adequacy, of the school's improvement since the last inspection;

- whether the school might be underachieving, have serious weaknesses, or require special measures.

62 In considering the pre-inspection information, do not lose sight of the wood for the trees. Ensure that the *Pre-Inspection Commentary* paints the 'big picture' of the school, and that the central hypotheses about the school stand out clearly. Effective *Pre-Inspection Commentaries* for both SHORT and FULL INSPECTIONS:

- draw on the full range of pre-inspection evidence, including the school's self-evaluation, views formed during the pre-inspection visit, parents' views and returned questionnaires;

- make full use of the *PICSI* data and the comparative figures in the *PICSI* annexes;

- build substantially on the issues raised in the previous inspection report; and the school's actions in response to them;

- provide an accurate historical analysis of the school's achievements and trends;

- identify hypotheses for further exploration or confirmation: issues for inspection.

STEP 12: TEAM BRIEFING AND MEETING

63   The team should meet for a final briefing before starting the inspection. You should note that:

- this is more than a short gathering before the first morning's inspection begins. A thorough briefing is required;

- it could be a morning meeting prior to beginning the inspection in the afternoon, or a separate meeting before the first day of the inspection;

- the meeting must not encroach on inspection time;

- the meeting should be for the whole inspection team, and where any team member begins the inspection at a later stage, arrangements must be made for a thorough briefing at that stage.

64   As the registered inspector, you will check the background and strengths of the team, if you do not already know them, and then:

- brief the team about the school and the *Pre-Inspection Commentary*;

- alert the team to any concerns or anxieties felt by the school or staff;

- ensure that all members of the team gather evidence against all the schedule headings;

- ensure that all members of the team know exactly what their first day's programme is to be;

- on FULL INSPECTIONS, ensure they have completed their subject *Pre-Inspection Commentaries*;

- clarify organisation and administrative arrangements;

- ensure that all are clear about their expected conduct.

65   You should make sure that the team is aware of all the issues and how these are to be tracked through. But above all, inspectors need to be aware of the 'big issues'. For example, if there is a strong boy/girl difference in test results, this should be clearly stated so that inspectors reflect their relative performance in each *Evidence Form* they write. The team should understand the school almost as well as you do by the end of the briefing.

DURING THE INSPECTION

THE ROLE OF THE REGISTERED INSPECTOR

66 As the registered inspector, you are the manager of the inspection team and the whole inspection process, and the first point of reference for everyone involved in the inspection. Effective management and organisation of the team on a day-to-day basis are crucial to the success of the inspection. It is your responsibility to ensure that judgements about the school are fair and accurate, are based on secure and representative evidence, comprehensively cover the schedule and contract requirements, and are corporately agreed. You are responsible for drawing key judgements together in the *Record of Corporate Judgements*.

67 You should:

- ensure that inspectors are consistent in their approaches to collecting and recording evidence and in how they conduct themselves and provide feedback to teachers;

- be prepared to adjust the patterns of work of individual inspectors as circumstances dictate;

- monitor and, if necessary, intervene in the work of the team to ensure compliance with the Framework and secure the necessary quality of evidence and judgements;

- undertake direct inspection such as observing work in classrooms, sampling pupils' written work, and holding discussions with staff, governors and pupils;

- keep a careful check on the sampling of the school's work and the extent of observation of individual teachers.

TEAM INSPECTORS' ASSIGNMENTS

68 Inspectors need to plan and use their time carefully and efficiently to achieve the coverage required, but they should be sensitive to the impact of the inspection on teachers and other staff in the school. Inspecting and evaluating the following aspects of the school's work will require contributions from the whole team but will need to be co-ordinated by one inspector:

- the quality of provision for pupils with special educational needs and the standards achieved by them;

- equality of opportunity for different groups of pupils;

- pupils' spiritual, moral, social and cultural development.

69 In FULL INSPECTIONS, inspectors need to draw evidence relating to their subject from across the curriculum. So, for example, the inspector leading on the inspection of English will need to take account of pupils' literacy skills and opportunities for developing these competencies in subjects other than English. This will require other inspectors to contribute. The same is true for mathematics, in relation to numeracy skills, and information technology. In these cases, the inspector taking the lead will need evidence from across the curriculum.

70   Team meetings are an essential part of any inspection. They allow contributions from all inspectors and generate a sense of common purpose based on good working relationships, and a clear understanding of everyone's responsibilities within the team. As the registered inspector, you should structure and manage these meetings to provide opportunities for:

- the proper consideration and exchange of inspection evidence and inspectors' views;

- discussion of emerging issues which require the attention of the whole team;

- the resolution of issues for inspection identified in the *Pre-Inspection Commentary*;

- discussion of any gaps or weaknesses in the evidence base and how to fill them;

- debate about evidence, views and judgements to ensure consistency and to resolve any conflicts where they arise.

71   It is good practice to establish a programme of team meetings with clear agendas before the inspection begins. You will need to build in some flexibility to take account of any emerging issues during the inspection. Team meetings must not encroach on inspection time.

GATHERING THE INSPECTION EVIDENCE

72   Within their assignments on FULL INSPECTIONS, individual inspectors must be allocated time to collect evidence on all parts of the *Evaluation Schedule*, so that they can contribute to the team's corporate judgements. They must also ensure they have enough evidence to form judgements in their own subjects. The evidence includes:

- the inspection of teaching and of pupils at work in classrooms and other areas; and work off-site where the inspection priorities allow, where there is agreement with the 'appropriate authority', and where it is practicable and manageable;

- discussions with pupils, for example, to assess their understanding and knowledge of different subjects and their attitudes to work and their life at school;

- the analysis of samples of pupils' work within individual subjects and across the curriculum;

- discussions with staff, especially those with management responsibilities, such as heads of department and heads of year;

- documentary analysis of schemes of work and teachers' plans, together with records of National Curriculum tests and teachers' assessments, any assessment undertaken of attainment on entry, GCSE, GNVQ, Advanced level and other examination results, and other measures or indicators of attainment and progress used by the school;

- the analysis of statements of special educational needs, annual and transitional reviews and individual education plans.

73   The evidence should be recorded on *Evidence Forms* and summarised in *Inspection Notebooks* as the inspection proceeds.

74   In SHORT INSPECTIONS, **all** inspectors will collect evidence, mainly from observation of lessons, across all relevant parts of the *Evaluation Schedule*. Individual inspectors will be assigned during the inspection to follow up particular issues, often through discussions, and will need to report these back to the rest of the team at team meetings. You should try to avoid undertaking too much documentary analysis in a SHORT INSPECTION. Confine this to those areas where there are particular strengths or weaknesses, to follow up why things are the way they are. The evidence should be recorded on *Evidence Forms*. If you choose to do so, you can use *Inspection Notebooks* to help you record your views and judgements and to structure your contribution to team meetings.

OBSERVATION OF LESSONS AND OTHER ACTIVITIES

75   While the school is in session the inspection team should aim to spend at least 60 per cent of its time observing lessons and sampling pupils' work. The time spent in lessons will vary, but some whole lessons must be observed. Lessons or sessions observed should be from the school's normal programme of work. Inspectors should not require changes to that programme.

76   In SHORT INSPECTIONS the sample of lessons should provide a cross-section of the work of the school. You should focus on the beginnings and ends of Key Stages, in particular Years 9 and 11, and at the end of courses in the sixth form. You should select the sample to include observation of the teaching of those teachers who hold management and/or subject responsibility, such as heads of subject departments and heads of year teaching lessons in personal and social education.

77   In FULL INSPECTIONS lesson observations should include sufficient work in each Key Stage. Inspectors should spend enough time in lessons to enable them to make valid and reliable judgements on standards, teaching and learning. There should be a particular focus on the attainment of the oldest pupils. You must aim to observe each teacher present in the school during the inspection at least once.

78   You should ensure that adequate time is allowed to inspect the full range of subjects taught in the sixth form.

79   Effective inspection involves looking at the work of individual pupils and discussing it with them. It also entails careful observation of teaching, including the organisation of work for pupils as a class, in groups or individually. Both need to be done so as not to disrupt either teaching or learning, and the taking of notes should be as unobtrusive as possible.

80   The load on teachers should be spread as evenly as possible. Wherever possible, teachers should not be kept waiting for their first visit from an inspector until near the end of the inspection. Inspectors should visit classes taught by supply teachers who are in the school for more than one day, and trainee teachers.

81   There should not normally be more than one inspector in a class at any time unless the class teacher agrees and there is a particular reason for it. An example would be to track the progress of a pupil with special educational needs, or where the registered inspector monitors the work of team members.

82   Inspection should include assemblies, extra-curricular activities, including sport if offered, and registration periods. It may also include fieldwork and educational visits where justifiable and practicable.

TALKING WITH PUPILS

83 Talking to pupils is a good source of evidence about what they know, can do and understand. It is particularly helpful in judging the extent of their understanding of current and recent work, and their ability to apply knowledge in different contexts. These discussions should take place as inspectors join individual pupils or groups of pupils at work in lessons. You should also use every opportunity to talk to pupils outside lessons, to find out their views of the school, their attitudes, their interests and the extent to which these are supported or fulfilled.

84 In all observation, it is important to listen to pupils':

- incidental talk and comments;

- contributions in class;

- responses to questions;

- questions, initiated by them;

- views, feelings and comments expressed in discussions.

THE ANALYSIS OF PUPILS' WORK

85 Pupils' earlier and current work provides an essential source of evidence of their attainment and progress. It also offers an insight into the curriculum, teaching and pupils' attitudes to work. You will need to look at samples of work. The nature of the samples should be agreed with the headteacher during the preliminary visit.

86 It is helpful if the analysis takes place near the beginning of the inspection. Importantly, it will help the team to form an early view of the standards achieved. In each subject, the review and analysis of pupils' work needs to establish whether the standards of the oldest pupils in each Key Stage mirror what the performance data show. This will help you to see what pupils do well and not so well.

87 In SHORT INSPECTIONS the sample should include:

- the work of pupils in Years 7, 9 and 11 in the core subjects. The sample in each of these year groups should include two pupils from those pupils of above-average, average and below-average attainment as interpreted by the school;

- a sample of work of pupils with statements of special educational needs.

88 In FULL INSPECTIONS, the sample should include:

- the work of pupils in all year groups in all subjects (including the sixth form). The sample in each year should include two pupils from each group of pupils of above-average, average and below-average attainment;

- the work of all pupils with statements of special educational needs.

89   For each pupil, examples of past and present work should be available in order to establish the range of work covered over time and to evaluate evidence of progress. Inspectors will find it helpful to have pupils' records available alongside their written work, including individual education plans or statements of special educational needs.

90   The evidence from analysing samples of work provides substantial confirmation of attainment and the breadth, depth and consolidation of learning. Other examples of pupils' work in classrooms, in exercise books or on display help to establish how representative the sample is.

DISCUSSION WITH STAFF, THE 'APPROPRIATE AUTHORITY' AND OTHERS INVOLVED IN THE WORK OF THE SCHOOL

91   Headteachers and registered inspectors alike value a daily meeting to agree administrative details, discuss any matters of concern, clarify inspection issues and obtain further information. These meetings contribute a great deal to the smooth running of an inspection and the maintenance of good relationships by sharing emerging hypotheses, providing the opportunity for the school to offer further evidence, and preparing the way for some of the judgements made at the end of the inspection.

92   Discussions with the headteacher, representatives of the 'appropriate authority', staff with particular management responsibilities and subject teachers provide important sources of evidence relating to roles and responsibilities, procedures and policies. They are essential to the professional dialogue between staff and inspectors, which contributes to the usefulness of inspection to schools. These discussions also help inspectors establish the context for their observations.

93   Discussion with teachers, especially at the end of lessons or sessions, is desirable, but it may not always be possible to have more than a brief exchange. However, the work of teachers should be acknowledged and as many opportunities as possible found for professional dialogue. Such dialogue might involve clarifying the context of the lesson or session, and of future work, as well as providing a brief evaluation of the quality of work seen, where this is possible. In SHORT INSPECTIONS the discussion at the end of, or shortly after, the lesson should provide brief feedback whenever possible on the quality of the teaching observed and any significant strengths and weaknesses.

94   You should arrange to meet staff and representatives of the 'appropriate authority' to discuss their areas of responsibility at mutually convenient times. This is best arranged by negotiation before the inspection starts. Where possible you should indicate the points you wish to raise in the discussion, giving those concerned time to think about the issues. You should not offer a pro forma which teachers may feel under extra pressure to prepare for and complete. Take care that meetings do not make unreasonable demands on teachers' time, for instance their break times. To ensure efficient use of teachers' and inspectors' time, you should plan and co-ordinate carefully the meetings with staff who have several responsibilities. Discussions with support staff, voluntary helpers and any visiting specialists, for example speech therapists, are also a valuable source of information and contribute to involving all staff in a FULL INSPECTION. It will not be possible to do this to the same extent on a SHORT INSPECTION.

THE PLACE OF DOCUMENTARY EVIDENCE

95 Schools should be judged primarily by their achievements, and on the effectiveness of their teaching, leadership and management in contributing to pupils' progress. Where a school is very effective, there is little need to trawl through all its procedural documents.

96 In the past, schools have spent an inordinate amount of time in preparing policies and revising curriculum plans or schemes, largely because of a forthcoming inspection. We wish to discourage this practice. Secondary schools are required by regulations to have a number of procedures and policies in place; other policies are simply recommended or encouraged by the DfEE or other national organisations. The presence or absence of non-statutory policies or documents is not intrinsically material to the quality and standards of the school. For example, a school is unremarkable if it achieves good attendance in a situation where you would expect attendance to be good. Where attendance is surprisingly good or is unsatisfactory, then you should investigate either why the school has achieved such unusually high attendance or, conversely, the reasons for attendance being poor, and what the school is doing or has done about it. In either of these cases, it is appropriate to look into the school's policy and procedures in respect of attendance, the way it handles absence, the dealings it has with parents over the question of attendance, and so on. A school should not be marked down simply for not having an attendance policy, unless the absence of such a policy, for example in a school with poor attendance, indicates a measure of complacency in dealing with the issue.

97 In all inspections, schools are asked to complete a school self-audit (*Form S3*). The school is not expected to undertake extensive audit activities in order to do this; it would normally be sufficiently well informed about what is required and how it meets those requirements. The form illustrates a range of areas in which statutory requirements apply to all or some schools. You should know what these requirements are.

98 In a SHORT INSPECTION, the small scale of the inspection means that only if a concern is raised during the inspection will the inspection team explore the school's compliance with the detail of statutory requirements. In a FULL INSPECTION, however, one or more inspectors from the team should follow up the school's compliance in a range of areas as part of, and relevant to, their responsibilities.

99 In a SHORT INSPECTION, inspectors should sample the planning which underpins some of the lessons they see, but should not *unless there is a significant concern* call for and inspect all the school's plans or schemes of work for different subjects. Nor should they ask for policy or operational documents unless they are material to the investigation of particular strengths and weaknesses.

100 In a FULL INSPECTION, inspectors should not require a school to produce voluminous documentation in advance of the inspection. They should look at the plans or schemes for the subjects they are inspecting as they exist in the school, either before or at an early stage in the inspection. The burden on schools of writing or photocopying must be kept to an *absolute* minimum, and schools should be reimbursed for any copying costs.

DISCUSSING YOUR FINDINGS WITH TEACHERS AND OTHER PARTIES

101   How well the messages given during feedback are received and acted upon depends much on the trust, respect and rapport established between you and the headteacher and staff during the inspection. The way you communicate findings is also important. You should therefore:

■ **gain teachers' acceptance;**

This includes talking with the teachers and other staff about their work as the inspection develops, showing sensitivity in your dealings with them and their pupils as evidence is collected, and interacting with the pupils as much as possible – though discreetly – during lesson observations.

■ **consider the effects of non-verbal as well as verbal messages during feedback and at other times.**

Eye contact and appropriate facial expression, posture, gesture, voice, pace and tone can all help to reduce anxiety, gain acceptance of inspection findings, and encourage constructive professional dialogue. Oral messages and body language should always be compatible.

102   You should offer feedback to every teacher observed. The objective is to help improve the teacher's effectiveness. You should try, whenever possible, to give firsthand feedback on the lessons you observe. The purpose is to let teachers know your perception of the quality of the lessons and responses of pupils: what went well; what was less successful; and what could be done more effectively. Feedback should therefore:

■ **identify the most important strengths and weaknesses in the teaching observed;**

You must be selective in what you say and not simply rehearse everything that you have seen. Illustrate general conclusions with specific and practical examples from the evidence you have. You should not strive to find weaknesses in teaching that has none.

■ **provide clear reasons for what you judged to be successful or otherwise;**

Strengths and weaknesses should always be linked to their effects on pupils' learning, and must be attributed to the teaching approaches used rather than the teacher.

■ **ensure that points for development are identified.**

Where the teaching is less than satisfactory, you should diagnose precisely what is not working and spell out what is needed to bring about improvement. It is equally important to identify how satisfactory and good teaching can be improved. You should, of course, acknowledge very good teaching and the features that make it so, but even here it is helpful if more subtle improvements can be identified.

FEEDBACK ON LESSONS

103   Where teaching is effective, feedback can usually be managed successfully after lessons – either at the end of the lesson if this is possible, or at a later time during the day if this is more convenient. Where there are concerns, you may need time to reflect upon what you have seen and, more particularly, upon how you might best discuss your findings with the teacher concerned. It is helpful to see more than one lesson before feeding back about unsatisfactory teaching, to gauge whether weaknesses are sustained.

104   In a SHORT INSPECTION, the team is unlikely to be able to see a sufficient sample of the work of all teachers to give a view of the overall quality of their teaching. Some will not be seen teaching; others may only be visited for a single lesson. In very effective schools, one expects to see few, if any, weaknesses in the teaching. You are not required to provide summary feedback to teachers towards or at the end of the inspection but you should give whatever feedback you can as you go along. In SHORT INSPECTIONS, teachers will not be given a profile of the judgements on their teaching.

105   In a FULL INSPECTION you should offer teachers summary feedback on the teaching that has been observed. Towards the end of the inspection, strengths and weaknesses in what has been seen can be pulled together. More than one inspector may have seen the work of an individual teacher. So the summary feedback to each teacher at the end of the inspection needs to be carefully co-ordinated to ensure that the inspector responsible for the feedback is well informed. Wherever possible, the inspector who is assigned to give feedback to a particular teacher should be the one who is best placed, by virtue of expertise or firsthand evidence collected, to make the greatest contribution to the professional development of that teacher. At the end of the inspection, each teacher is given a written record of the inspectors' judgements of their teaching, with a copy to the headteacher.

106   The requirement for individual performance feedback applies to:

- full-time and part-time teachers;

- supply teachers, except those working for less than five days in the school;

- teachers funded under Ethnic Minorities Achievement Grant (EMAG) and other grants for specific purposes;

- others such as qualified support teachers, where they are responsible for classes or groups of children or the focus of evaluation of teaching has been on their work.

107   The requirement to provide individual performance feedback does not apply to the following staff and helpers, although you should offer it where possible. These staff are not given the written profile of judgements about their teaching, where their work was the focus of observation. However, you should include as many of these people as possible in ongoing dialogue. Their recorded work will be collated under a composite heading OTHER CONTRIBUTIONS TO TEACHING in the profile given to the headteacher. The profile of judgements is not given to:

- trainee teachers;

- special needs support assistants;

- non-teaching support assistants;

- artists and writers in residence;

■ instructors and coaches;

■ visitors and other voluntary helpers.

FEEDBACK TO HEADS OF DEPARTMENTS

108   Feedback to those with management responsibility for subjects or key aspects of the school's work is essential. Usually there is 'drip-feeding' of evaluations and sharing of hypotheses during the inspection, and summary feedback at the end of the week. There should be no major surprises at the end of the inspection. The summary feedback should:

■ present the significant inspection findings supported by sufficient evidence so that the reasons for judgements are understood;

■ provide an opportunity to clarify the findings;

■ explore areas of disagreement;

■ examine priorities for action;

■ give the head of department a clear basis on which to start planning for improvement.

109   In a SHORT INSPECTION, you are unlikely to see a large enough sample of work to come to unequivocal views of quality and standards in all the subjects of the curriculum. In these circumstances, and taking account of the brevity of the inspection, you are not required to offer feedback to subject heads of departments at the end of the inspection. It is enough to do what you can as you go along.

110   In a FULL INSPECTION, feedback should be given to as many heads of departments as possible. It should give them a clear picture of the inspection findings in their subject. In particular, it should rehearse the significant evidence and judgements about:

■ standards in the subject;

■ the quality of teaching and learning in the subject;

■ improvement since the last inspection;

■ areas identified as particular strengths and weaknesses;

■ issues identified by inspection as priorities for improving the school.

THE FINAL TEAM MEETING

111   The main purpose of this team meeting is to arrive at accurate and thoroughly secure corporate judgements about the school, recording these in the *Record of Corporate Judgements*. You, as the registered inspector, need to manage this meeting so that the hypotheses tested out during the inspection are discussed and conclusions reached. You need to bring judgements together so that the culmination of the meeting is the team's overall view of the effectiveness of the school. The strengths and weaknesses recorded in WHAT THE SCHOOL DOES WELL and WHAT COULD BE IMPROVED also need to be specifically agreed by the team.

112   Therefore, all inspectors need to have reflected on their evidence, to have reached their own views, and to be prepared to contribute these at the meeting. This means the meeting must not take place immediately after the inspection finishes. If the inspection finishes at lunchtime, you will need time to complete your *Inspection Notebook* in a FULL INSPECTION, or to gather your thoughts together in a SHORT INSPECTION before a meeting later in the afternoon. If the inspection finishes at the end of the school day, the final team meeting must not be held that day.

113   The meeting must be structured to achieve the goals set out above. In particular, the following areas must be included:

- discussions leading to the completion of the *Record of Corporate Judgements*;

- agreement about the contents of the summary of the inspection report;

- consideration, as a team, whether the school is in need of special measures, has serious weaknesses or is underachieving.

114   We expect that all inspectors will attend this team meeting. We recognise that there will be exceptional circumstances where this is not possible. If that is the case, the inspector concerned must provide the registered inspector with his/her completed *Inspection Notebook* (except the draft text for the report) and any additional points that need to be brought to the attention of other inspectors.

FEEDBACK TO THE HEADTEACHER AND SENIOR STAFF

115   Your feedback should give senior management an early but firm basis on which to start planning in response to the inspection's findings. In particular, the feedback to senior management should rehearse the significant evidence and judgements about:

- the school's outcomes, particularly standards achieved by pupils;

- the factors which most account for what is achieved, particularly the strengths and weaknesses in teaching in the school;

- the effectiveness of work done by managers and heads of departments;

- the issues identified by inspection as priorities for improving the school.

116   The staff attending the meeting should have the opportunity to clarify any of these findings, ask for further examples of evidence on which particular judgements about the school are based, and explore with inspectors the priorities for action.

117   The feedback to the headteacher and invited staff must be after the inspection has finished. It must not be on the last day of the inspection or even the day after. As the registered inspector, you must leave sufficient time to reflect on the evidence and corporate judgements in order to prepare properly.

118   The headteacher can invite whom he or she wishes to the feedback meeting, but it is usually for the senior management team only. No one other than the staff of the school should normally attend. There may be exceptional circumstances when the presence of an LEA officer as an observer is justified, for example:

- if the school has a temporary headteacher pending a permanent appointment;

- if the headteacher is judged likely to find the inspection findings distressing.

119   In such exceptional circumstances, the school can invite the officer only with the consent of the registered inspector.

120   The formal feedback should not be confused with the interim feedback offered to headteachers towards the end of an inspection by many registered inspectors. This is helpful to the school in relieving uncertainties and stress.

FEEDBACK TO THE 'APPROPRIATE AUTHORITY'

121   The success of the feedback to the 'appropriate authority', usually the governing body, hinges on how effectively inspectors communicate the main inspection findings clearly and frankly to a mixed audience, many of whom are well-informed but not professional teachers or educators. The same general principles apply to giving feedback to the governing body as to the senior management team, but the presentation to the governing body should have much less detail. The presentation should include a careful explanation of specific matters which should be included in the post-inspection plan. This is to ensure that the governing body is clear at an early stage about what the school should do to improve. It will often help to use visual aids to summarise the main points of the presentation.

122   The governing body for an LEA-maintained school may, if it wishes, invite an LEA officer (or diocesan education officer or similar religious adviser in the case of schools with a religious character) to be present as an observer at the oral feedback to the governing body. In most cases you will wish to include these observers in the dialogue. However, as the registered inspector, you may need to remind observers of their role if they become too assertive.

SOME GENERAL POINTS ABOUT FEEDBACK

123   Formal feedback meetings must take place before the inspection report is finished and as soon as is practicable after the inspection. The content of the oral feedback is confidential and the findings of the inspection should not be released, particularly to parents and the press, until after the 'appropriate authority' has received the report. You may wish to remind those attending these meetings of their confidentiality.

124   The quality of the feedback is an important factor in influencing how the school responds to the inspection findings, and particularly in drawing up its post-inspection action plan for improvement. Effective feedback:

- is well structured, clear, succinct and unrushed;

- makes use of appropriate visual aids to help communicate the inspection findings, especially to governing bodies;

- places greater emphasis on what the school does well and what could be improved, and why, but also covers the relevant reporting requirements in the *Evaluation Schedule*;

- presents a balanced and rounded picture of the school;

- gives well-chosen examples or observations that show you know the school;

- allows opportunities for discussion and clarification of the inspection findings;

- avoids giving detailed advice to the school about how to tackle the improvements that are needed.

125   It is expected that all oral reporting will proceed smoothly and professionally and that feedback will be of value to staff and governors alike. If, however, the behaviour of those at a feedback meeting makes it impossible to proceed with a sensible professional dialogue, you as the registered inspector have the right to confine the feedback simply to the main findings of the inspection and the key issues for action. In extreme cases, you have the right not to proceed with the oral report.

126   The use of tape recorders by headteachers, governing bodies and individual teachers at feedback meetings is entirely at the discretion of the registered inspector. It is reasonable for you not to proceed with a feedback meeting if there is any insistence on their use against your will. OFSTED has no objection to the tape recording of feedback meetings if the registered inspector agrees.

THE REPORT AND THE SUMMARY OF THE REPORT

STANDARDS OF REPORTING

127 The inspection report must be a carefully considered, clearly written and well-checked document of high quality. It must relay the inspection findings as unequivocal judgements in clear, straightforward language so that:

- parents, governors, the staff of the school and other readers get a clear picture of the quality and standards of the school, an understanding of its strengths and weaknesses, and insights into why the school achieves as it does;

- the school has a good basis for subsequent action to improve standards and the quality of education.

128 The report should reflect the individual school. It is unique to the school and must, on no account, duplicate in whole or in part the text of earlier reports, however similar the school. The report must follow the structure set out in the *Evaluation Schedule* but its content, wording and style should not be written to any pre-determined formula. Key judgements must be absolutely clear, and consistent with the oral feedback given to the school and governors. Reasons for judgements should be given to enable readers to understand why the inspection team has arrived at its views. While judgements should be based on the criteria set out in the *Evaluation Schedule*, the report should focus on strengths and areas where improvement is needed. It is not necessary to allude to each and every criterion in the schedule, nor to quote the criteria parrot-fashion.

129 It is essential that the report provides clear interpretations of any performance data and presents the inspection team's judgements about the educational standards achieved by pupils at the school. Overall judgements should be illustrated by reference to the strengths and weaknesses in the areas of learning or different subjects or courses of the curriculum.

130 The report must explain any apparent inconsistencies, for example where teaching is generally good but achievement is poor.

131 When reporting on the quality of education provided, inspectors must focus, in particular, on the quality of teaching and learning. Other aspects of provision are important only for their effect on the quality of teaching and learning and the educational standards achieved. Where those other aspects of provision are unexceptional, further justification is usually unnecessary. Where there are particular strengths and weaknesses, though, amplification is needed in order to explain why, for example, mathematics teaching is 'outstanding' or leadership is 'weak'.

132 The **summary report** and the section of the report on WHAT SHOULD THE SCHOOL DO TO IMPROVE FURTHER? are particularly important. The summary is the report for parents and needs particularly careful drafting to communicate effectively with a wide readership. It must draw out the key judgements about the school and leave it without any doubt about the strengths and weaknesses of the school. The contents of the summary, particularly the sections on WHAT THE SCHOOL DOES WELL and WHAT COULD BE IMPROVED, must be consistent with the rest of the report.

133 The report, and its summary, should therefore:

- be clear to all its readers, governors, parents, professionals and the public at large;

- concentrate on evaluating rather than describing what is seen;

- focus on the educational standards achieved and the factors which impact on standards and quality;

- use everyday language, not educational jargon, and be grammatically correct;

- be specific in its judgements;

- use sub-headings, bullet points and other devices where they help to make the messages clear;

- use telling examples drawn from the evidence base to make generalisations understandable and to illustrate what is meant by 'good' or 'poor';

- employ words and phrases that enliven the report and convey the individual character of the school.

134 Readers of the summary report will not necessarily read the full report. The summary report must, therefore, be capable of standing alone as a fair and balanced picture of the school, and the steps needed to improve it.

135 The summary report must include the elements specified in the *Evaluation Schedule*. In addition, the summary report must include the standard text specified in the report template issued to inspectors.

136 The report and summary of the report must be produced within six calendar weeks from the end of the inspection and forwarded without delay to the 'appropriate authority', HMCI and persons specified in sections 16 and 20 of the 1996 Act. The 'appropriate authority' must previously have had five working days to comment on the draft version of the report.

STRUCTURE OF REPORTS

137 The structure is shown schematically on page 136. All inspection reports include the summary of the report (Part A), the commentary (Part B) and a data section (Part C). **Reports of FULL INSPECTIONS also include a subject section (Part D). Reports of SHORT and FULL INSPECTIONS differ markedly in the structure of the commentary.**

138 In SHORT INSPECTIONS, the commentary is based on the two sections of the summary entitled WHAT THE SCHOOL DOES WELL and WHAT COULD BE IMPROVED. Each of the strengths and weaknesses listed in these two sections of the summary becomes a sub-heading of the commentary. For example, if the first item in WHAT THE SCHOOL DOES WELL is: 'Pupils' speaking and listening skills are excellent', then this finding becomes the first sub-heading for the commentary. The commentary of short reports, therefore, does not follow the headings provided by the *Evaluation Schedule*.

139 In FULL INSPECTIONS, the commentary of the report follows the structure set out in the *Evaluation Schedule*.

PRESENTATION OF THE PRE-PUBLICATION REPORT TO THE SCHOOL

140   The school has five working days in which to consider the final, pre-publication draft of the inspection report to check the factual accuracy of its content. *The registered inspector must ensure that the report shown to the school is his or her intended final report and is of publication quality. By this stage it must have taken account of comments made by any editorial reader hired by the contractor.* Showing this report to the school is not meant to be an opportunity to negotiate judgements. The report should contain no surprises. It should reflect precisely the judgements conveyed during oral feedback to the senior managers and the 'appropriate authority'.

REPORTING REQUIREMENTS

REPORT

SUMMARY + COMMENTARY

THIS IS PART A OF THE REPORT

- Information about the school
- How good the school is

followed by a list of the main strengths of the school and any weaknesses under the headings:

- What the school does well
- What could be improved

If the school is judged to be underachieving, or is identified as having serious weaknesses or requiring special measures, this should be stated.

- How the school has improved since its last inspection
- Standards
- Pupils' attitudes and values
- Teaching and learning
- Other aspects of the school
- How well is the school led and managed?
- Parents' and carers' views of the school

The summary report must include:

- all statutory reporting requirements;
- required judgements about each of the ☐ headings for sections 1–9 of the *Evaluation Schedule* and, in FULL INSPECTIONS, a summary of the strengths and weaknesses from section 10 of the *Schedule*.

SHORT INSPECTION

FULL INSPECTION

THIS IS PART B OF THE REPORT

A commentary on each of the issues listed in:

- What the school does well
  and
- What could be improved?

  followed by sections on:

- What should the school do to improve further?
- Other specified features (if any)

THIS IS PART C OF THE REPORT

Data tables

Summary of responses to parents' questionnaire

THIS IS PART B OF THE REPORT

- How high are the standards?
  The school's results and pupils' achievements
  Pupils' attitudes, values and personal development
- How well are pupils taught?
- How good are the curricular and other opportunities offered to pupils?
- How well does the school care for its pupils?
- How well does the school work in partnership with parents?
- How well is the school led and managed?
- What should the school do to improve further?
- Other specified features (if any)

THIS IS PART C OF THE REPORT

Data tables

Summary of responses to parents' questionnaire

THIS IS PART D OF THE REPORT

- The standards and quality of teaching in areas of the curriculum and subjects

PART 3

USING THE *HANDBOOK* FOR SCHOOL SELF-EVALUATION

SELF-EVALUATION

The school that knows and understands itself is well on the way to solving any problems it has. The school that is ignorant of its weaknesses or will not, or cannot, face up to them is not well-managed. Self-evaluation provides the key to improvement. The ability to generate a commitment among staff to appraise their own work critically, and that of others, is a key test of how well a school is managed.

Effective change and self-evaluation are characterised by openness and consultation and are a regular part of the good school's working life in which everyone is encouraged to participate. Self-evaluation complements inspection with a constant process of identifying priorities for improvement, monitoring provision and evaluating outcomes.

Both inspection and internal evaluation are concerned with providing an accurate appraisal of the quality and standards of the school and diagnosing what needs to be done to improve them. Inspectors have a duty to report, via the governing body, to parents. Schools are encouraged to do the same with their self-evaluation findings.

It is advantageous to base school self-evaluation on the same criteria as those used in all schools by inspectors. A common language has developed about the work of schools, expressed through the criteria. Teachers and governors know that the criteria reflect things that matter.

The guidance on inspection published for inspectors in the first revision of the OFSTED *Handbooks*[2] is accepted by headteachers as a sound basis for evaluation, defining a useful range of criteria to assess the quality and impact of what schools provide for pupils. *School Evaluation Matters*[3] exemplifies and illustrates the work of many schools for whom monitoring and evaluation are central to improvement. *Making the Most of Inspection*[4] helps schools to see external inspection as one aspect of evaluation, which can be actively used to promote improvement.

Self-evaluation is not about being an inspector. By using this guidance you should be able to undertake an annual analysis of the standards and the effectiveness of your actions.

There are four questions that are at the heart of evaluating everything you do:

- **Are all the pupils in my school learning as much as they are capable of learning?**

- **What can I do to find out?**

- **When I answer this question how do I know I am right?**

- **What do I do about it when I have the answer?**

---

[2] The OFSTED *Handbooks: Guidance on the Inspection of Nursery, Primary, Secondary and Special Schools,* HMSO 1995.

[3] OFSTED Publications Centre 1998.

[4] OFSTED Publications Centre 1998.

To ensure that self-evaluation has the maximum impact on standards:

- take an objective look at pupils' achievements and pinpoint areas of underachievement;

- account for outcomes in your school by identifying strengths and weaknesses in teaching, before looking at what else you provide to support learning;

- use this information to devise the School Improvement (Development) Plan, which is at its best when seen simply as a means to raise standards.

WHAT POINT HAVE YOU REACHED?

In 1997–98 one in three of all schools was judged to be good, or very good, at monitoring and evaluating the quality of its work, and a further one in three was judged to be satisfactory. The remaining one-third were unsatisfactory. Primary schools were generally slightly better at this than secondary schools. Although these proportions show an improvement since the beginning of the OFSTED inspection cycle, there is still much work to be done.[5]

Secondary schools vary in their management of evaluation. For example, in one secondary school:

The headteacher and deputies each take responsibility for evaluating the performance of several departments. They observe teaching to supplement that undertaken by the head of department. They undertake a periodic review of each department and validate the departmental self-evaluation. They hold each department responsible for monitoring and improving the performance of both pupils and staff. The senior management group reports annually to governors on the strengths and weaknesses of the school's performance.

School self-evaluation is about diagnosis and change in the way people work, and this is particularly so for teaching and its impact. But it must carry a 'health warning'. It can be a mistake to 'do a self-evaluation' of the whole school, treating it as one event like 'having an inspection'. It is far better that inspection complements a process of identifying and nibbling away at priorities through regular monitoring and evaluation.

- **If you have not introduced a strategy for monitoring and evaluating** the work of your school, your area of responsibility, or your own work in the classroom, you will find the *Handbook* particularly helpful.

- **If some monitoring and evaluation is in place,** this guidance will enable you to assess how effectively you undertake it.

- **If you feel there is already 'continuous evaluation',** you will be able to check whether such blanket coverage is concealing some prime suspects for investigation.

- **If you feel there is little we can tell you about self-evaluation,** then we should be pleased if you would tell us more about what you do.

Wherever you are up to, *Form S4* (on the CD-ROM attached to this *Handbook*) is about self-evaluation. It is for the inspection team, but we believe that many headteachers and governors will find *Form S4* a useful basis for the regular evaluation of the progress their school is making, across all its work, whether or not it is being inspected.

---

[5]   Data taken from *Primary Education 1994–98*, HMSO 1999; and *Secondary Education 1993–97*, HMSO 1998.

WHERE DO YOU BEGIN?

There are several possible starting points. They may include:

■ **areas identified by senior management or the governing body as needing improvement;**

> which may have arisen as a result of monitoring performance, evidence of problems, a survey of parents or staff, or for other reasons;

■ **interest by one or more particular staff;**

> in which case they should be helped and encouraged, and their work used as a pilot for wider adoption;

■ **a known area of strength or weakness in the school;**

> which can then be evaluated and the reasons for success or lack of it diagnosed;

■ **an inspection report;**

> in which issues are identified that need to be investigated further as a basis for action.

Two of the most systematic spurs to self-evaluation are the appraisal of teachers, and the monitoring and analysis of performance. Inspectors start from the latter point, as illustrated in Part 2 of this *Handbook*. Monitoring and analysing performance have the advantage of illuminating where to focus your evaluative effort. Appraisal, on the other hand, applies to all and is a major undertaking.

EVALUATING STANDARDS

Start with monitoring standards and related matters. Strong internal reviews look first at key measurable outcomes. Your monitoring of measurable outcomes, such as standards, should result in evaluation that examines the quality and impact of what you provide. For instance, use:

■ baseline data of attainment on entry;

■ analysis of test and examination results and teacher assessments;

■ a study of ethnicity and gender balances in your results;

■ test analysis;

■ monitoring to know how many pupils reach their performance targets;

■ standards in the school measured against other schools;

■ value-added information;

■ an analysis of pupils' work by pupil type and across Key Stages;

■ an analysis of attendance and punctuality patterns;

■ interviews with staff about their classes;

■ a review of governors' attitudes to standards in your school;

■ questions to parents about what they think of what your school does.

You will want to: analyse standards on entry; predict the maximum possible gains in knowledge, understanding and skills for pupils and set appropriate goals; determine how these can best be achieved; analyse performance at the end of each year and key stage; record the progress made by pupils, and decide where, if anywhere, improvements are needed.

Your *Performance and Assessment Report (PANDA)* provides data to help answer the question: **How high are standards?** Your school is likely to have other data available, such as the results of standardised tests used for diagnostic purposes, baseline assessments, or value-added data. The guidance in section 2 of Part 1 of this *Handbook* will help steer you through the analytical process needed in order to form an objective view of the standards reached by your pupils, and whether or not pupils achieve as much as they should.

The data should give you a good picture of trends over time. It also shows relative achievements in the core subjects. Analysis of the data should prompt questions such as: *Why are so few pupils achieving level 5 in mathematics? Why is writing apparently so much weaker than reading? Why are results not better midway through Key Stage 2?*

The analysis of data, therefore, can provide an immediate focus for self-evaluation. You may start, for example, by looking carefully at the standard of work done or recorded by pupils to get a first indication of where strengths and weaknesses lie. Sometimes, one teacher may be unusually effective or ineffective in much of the work they do with their class. In the case of such weakness, evaluation of teaching becomes an appraisal of competence: a different issue.

EVALUATING TEACHING

The monitoring, evaluation and support of teaching are central to school effectiveness and improvement. Systematic monitoring of teaching through classroom observation is relatively rare. As a result, in many schools senior staff lack the knowledge they need if they are to help raise standards. The observation and evaluation of teaching and learning should be based on clear and understood criteria. Section 3 of Part 1 of this *Handbook* – HOW WELL ARE PUPILS TAUGHT? – gives national criteria for judging teaching and learning, together with guidance on their application.

The section entitled *Making Judgements* states clearly the characteristics of very good teaching and unsatisfactory teaching. You may initially want to focus on one subject or aspect of teaching.

You will see that the overriding consideration for evaluating the quality of teaching is how well pupils learn. This is judged not only by assessing their knowledge, understanding and skills, but by looking at the extent of their engagement in the lesson, the pace of their work and the demands made on them. If these are good, decide what are the features of teaching which have this effect. If the converse is true, you need to diagnose what is not working well enough and consider what could be done to improve matters. Evaluation and setting an agenda for development are starting points, but are of limited value unless the monitoring of classroom teaching is systematic; carried out to agreed criteria; and the outcomes discussed with teachers.

The section on *Guidance on using the Evaluation Schedule* helps you to know what to look for in your lesson observations. You can use the *Evaluation Forms* on the CD-ROM to record the information. Before the observation ensure that teachers know what your focus will be. Try to make sure that it arises from the monitoring you have done of standards. During lesson observations, record what teachers do well and less well, always judge their work by the impact it has on pupils' learning. Note how pupils respond during the lesson, watch how their attitudes to learning and their behaviour influence the standards they reach. Try to record how much learning has taken place during your observation, measured by talking with pupils, examining their work and looking back through their work to see where they have come from, and gauge their progress.

As you conclude an observation decide how effective the lesson was overall, which parts worked best and which – if any – did not work so well. Did all pupils in the class gain from the demands made of them? Did all the teaching techniques and elements of the lesson contribute well to the intended outcomes? Where were the strengths and weaknesses? What could be done more effectively in future?

FEEDING BACK AFTER OBSERVING LESSONS, AND ONGOING SUPPORT

It is essential to have an agreed format for feeding back your considered evaluation of teaching. Schools may use different ways of doing this. Some do it collectively, with the group of staff involved, others individually. The guidance provided for inspectors in Part 2 of this *Handbook*, on giving feedback, may be helpful to you.

Evaluation should lead to personal or team agendas for becoming more effective. These should include targets for improvement, against which progress may be monitored through regular structured follow-up observations to see if the targets have been realised. It is important that management supports these agendas in all possible ways, which may include professional development, the acquisition of resources and the opportunity to visit teachers in other classes or schools.

PERFORMANCE MANAGEMENT AND LEADING IMPROVEMENT

If you are a headteacher or governor in a maintained school, performance management is now an integral part of your work. The 1999 *School Teachers' Pay and Conditions Document*[6] stipulates that headteachers' professional duties include:

> *evaluating the standards of teaching and learning in the school, and ensuring that proper standards of professional performance are established and maintained.*

Many would argue that all staff with management responsibilities have similar obligations. Performance is rightly associated with the standards achieved and the quality of learning. Performance management policies will centre on the assessment of teaching, and analysis of pupils' progress and learning, to guide the setting of targets for improvement and development over the next year. The governing body has responsibility for appraising the performance of the headteacher, setting appropriate targets for the headteacher and deciding on performance-related pay for the headteacher and staff.

---

[6] *School Teachers' Pay and Conditions Document 1999*, paragraph 43.7.

Performance management is most effective where there is:

- strong, well-motivated and clear-sighted leadership;

- rigorous analysis of standards;

- continuous monitoring and evaluation of teaching and learning;

- wholehearted commitment from staff to the school and to self-improvement;

- a set of easily understood objectives and reasonable but challenging targets at all levels;

- plenty of support for development and improvement;

- good management of resources, including financial incentives and rewards that maximise performance.

The impact of your management and leadership and of those who support you in running the school will dictate how governors, staff, pupils and parents see the quality of your performance as the headteacher. The *Evaluation Schedule* section 7, HOW WELL IS THE SCHOOL LED AND MANAGED?, will help you to review and improve your own performance and that of any senior colleagues you may have. Remember that you may not be the best person to lead such an evaluation. Involve teachers new to the school, parents, governors and staff. Some schools also involve pupils in school evaluation. The section headed *Making Judgements* makes clear the vital features of good leaders and managers, and the section on leadership and management will help you to find ways of measuring the impact of what you and your colleagues do, and how it benefits pupils.

As the headteacher, you are strongly influential in providing a culture in which the cycle of self-evaluation and development is valued, understood, published and communicated. It is crucially important that you assure its effectiveness and ensure that everyone in the school is involved in, and committed to, their own learning as part of maximising pupils' achievements. Thus to be at your best you, your staff and governors should be reflective and analytical when weighing up the value, or effectiveness, of what you provide.

USING INSPECTION TO COMPLEMENT SELF-EVALUATION

Inspection, well used, complements good self-evaluation. During an inspection there will be a number of opportunities for you and your staff to: test your perceptions of the school against those of impartial, external evaluators; receive feedback; and discuss the quality and standards being achieved. Making the most of these opportunities, and the discussions and professional debates during the more formal feedback meetings, will provide additional valuable information to add to your own evaluation of your school. Together with the key issues, all these points will help you and your governors to prepare an action plan and direct your school improvement planning.

As with the outcomes of your self-evaluation activities, use inspection to celebrate success. It is essential to recognise where the school is doing well, and to compliment those involved, as well as to tackle matters that need to be improved. It is particularly important to be positive and forward-looking after the inspection is over and the report has arrived, or after any phase of intensive evaluation, in order to combat the sense of anticlimax which can prevail, even with the most resounding endorsement of the school.

SCHOOL SELF-EVALUATION IN A NUTSHELL

Start now

Accept that we can all improve

Place the raising of standards at the heart of all your planning

Measure standards

Compare yourself with others

Regularly observe each other teaching to a set of agreed and rigorous criteria

Evaluate the effect that teaching has on learning

Be completely open in feeding back what you find

Think, discuss and consult

Set targets for everyone's improvement

Ensure that action is supported, monitored and reviewed

Never stop evaluating

Example 1

Evaluation in an English department

Aware of the National Literacy Strategy, the head of English in a large, 11–16 secondary school has used five hours of non-teaching time each week for a month to interview a range of Key Stage 3 pupils about their reading. She was concerned to note that very few pupils were reading for pleasure; much reading was of magazines and non-fiction reference books and very few pupils carried reading books with them.

She sought firsthand evidence of what teachers in the department were doing to encourage pupils to broaden their reading.

After discussion with her staff, she decided that over the following two months she would observe all her staff teaching. The department studied the booklet Inspecting Subjects and Aspects 11–18 – English,[7] **looking particularly at the section on teaching, pages 7–9.** Her colleagues agreed that it would be particularly helpful to focus on the ways in which their teaching encouraged the reading of a range of texts, in particular, fiction.

A newly qualified teacher, who joined the department two terms previously, was charged to evaluate the use of the school library by Key Stage 3 pupils and the quality and range of the library provision at Key Stage 3 for fiction reading.

Some teachers in the department sought reassurance that the criteria on which their teaching was to be judged were made clear and that they would receive feedback. Everyone agreed that the observation would centre on four of the criteria for teaching (shown below as reworded in the new inspection Framework).

- Do teachers plan effectively, setting clear objectives that pupils understand?

- Do teachers challenge and inspire pupils, expecting the most of them, so as to deepen their knowledge and understanding?

- Do teachers use methods that enable all pupils to learn effectively?

- How well does the teaching meet the needs of all pupils?

These criteria were applied specifically to the teaching of reading. The head of department used the Observation (now Evidence) Form (see the CD-ROM) to record observations, a copy of which would be given to the teacher.

When the teaching was analysed it showed that:

- pupils gained the most pleasure from reading fiction where the level of books pupils read was well matched to their skills;

- pupils given the chance to talk about their reading to the teacher in class were more likely to read for pleasure;

- the newly appointed teacher took particular care to involve parents in pupils' reading, with some success;

- many pupils, particularly boys, did not see reading fiction as a way of helping them to do well in other subjects;

(continued overleaf)

---

[7] OFSTED Publications Centre 1999.

(Example continued)

- *32 per cent of Key Stage 3 pupils use the school library at least once a week and of these just half borrow books from the fiction section;*
- *Terry Pratchett books were the most popular, especially among the most capable readers (majority girls); hardly any pupils read newspapers, but many read magazines regularly (football, teenage lifestyle, computers).*

The head of department wrote a brief paper analysing these findings and invited the headteacher and the librarian to the department meetings set to discuss this monitoring exercise. As a result, a lively discussion ensued during which it was agreed that:

- *all teachers (not just a few) of Year 7 pupils would use Key Stage 2 and CATs assessment data to match the level of reading text to pupils' prior attainment;*

- *Year 8 and 9 teachers would also match the level of readers more closely to pupils' prior attainment;*

- *silent reading in class of individually chosen books would be used to monitor and extend reading skills by teachers, hearing all pupils read at least once a fortnight and recording their progress;*

- *pupils would be encouraged to read to each other in pairs;*

- *a working group would be set up to help introduce some aspects of the literacy hour into Key Stage 3 English lessons;*

- *a bid would be made for an injection of capital into the library to extend the range of fiction texts and strengthen the quality of non-fiction texts, particularly autobiography, biography and magazines;*

- *two teachers would examine ways of involving parents in the department's attempts to broaden reading skills, and pilot the setting of reading targets.*

A number of the English teachers found this process very helpful to them and it was agreed that a follow-up evaluation of progress on the development points would be made after eight teaching weeks, with the headteacher and head of English releasing the second in department to undertake the lesson observations.

PART 4

ANNEXES

ANNEX 1

JUDGING BEST VALUE PRINCIPLES AND FINANCIAL MANAGEMENT IN SCHOOLS

There is a statutory duty on local authorities (in general, not just LEAs) to obtain best value by securing economic, efficient and effective services. The best value framework, within which local authorities are required to respond to local needs and make decisions locally, primarily focuses on the balance between cost and quality in striving continuously to improve services.

The best value approach does not apply statutorily to governing bodies in their use of delegated and devolved budgets. However, governing bodies are required to set targets to raise standards, are expected to provide a good-quality public service, and spend public money wisely. Schools are accountable for balancing *costs* (in terms of economy and efficiency) and *effectiveness* (in terms of their performance and the quality of what they provide) as required by the best value framework. To achieve this schools need to demonstrate that they apply best value principles in arriving at decisions about all their activities, especially how the financial resources delegated to them are managed.

Your task on inspection is, in light of all the available evidence, to evaluate and report on how effectively the school applies best value principles in its management and use of resources.

INSPECTION AND THE BEST VALUE FRAMEWORK

Inspecting the use of the best value framework fits easily within the overall inspection process. Both require attention to be given to evaluating the school's performance and its management and planning processes. One sign of effective planning is, for example, a challenging and appropriately costed school development plan.

The best value framework covers *four principles* (summarised as the four 'C's), each of which is linked to specific requirements in the *Evaluation Schedule*:

- Compare;

- Challenge;

- Consult;

- Compete.

The following are examples of questions you may wish to use, grouped under the headings related to the four principles.

COMPARE: Comparison of performance against that of all schools and similar schools is readily possible for secondary schools. *PANDA reports* and other data provide suitable benchmarks and other indicators to enable the school to monitor its performance, measure it against others and set targets. Find out the extent to which the school asks itself, and answers, such questions as:

■ *What is the quality of education provided by similar schools?*

■ *How do our standards compare with theirs?*

■ *Are we a relatively high performer?*

■ *Do we cost more or less than others?*

■ *Why?*

Guidance on evaluating value for money appears in Part 1 of this *Handbook*.

CHALLENGE: This is about whether the school challenges itself about the services it provides. Does the school take steps, for example, to find out whether what it provides is what is needed, within the discretion allowed in the statutory framework for the curriculum and outside the statutory minimum? In secondary schools, there is a diverse range of provision from 14 to 16 or 18 years. Is it the best provision that could be made for those students? Does the introduction of a new course fulfil the conditions of best value? Is sixth form provision right for the students? Is it cost-effective? Could some of it be provided better elsewhere? Find out the extent to which the school asks itself such questions as:

■ *Why are we doing this?*

■ *Is it what people want?*

■ *What is the evidence about level of need?*

■ *Could someone else do it differently, or better?*

CONSULT: This is about being clear what the school community wants. When considering major changes or spending decisions, involving the curriculum provided or other major developments, does the school seek the views of those most concerned, and how does it respond to those views? This means asking or getting feedback from staff, parents, pupils and others on:

■ *what they want the school to do;*

■ *what they think of proposed changes or major expenditure;*

■ *whether they are happy with, or at, the school;*

■ *what is in their best interests.*

Did the school consult parents, for example, when drawing up a post-inspection action plan? or when changing the balance of the curriculum? Or does it just announce such matters? Increasingly, schools use questionnaires to survey parents; many also periodically seek the views of pupils. Many secondary schools have a pupils' council. Can it take real decisions and express a customer's view of the school? Is there a mechanism for pupils or students to express a view on teaching?

COMPETE: Competition is concerned both with whether the school is doing anything which could be better provided by someone else, and with the strategic use of resources and getting best value for expenditure. Does the school have proper financial administration procedures, including competitive tendering for significant expenditure? Examples might include supply and part-time staff, in-service training, expenditure on equipment and maintenance contracts. Is purchasing on a fair and open basis or through personal connection, or is one supplier used regardless of price? The school should be asking questions like:

■ *Are we providing the service at the right price?*

■ *Could we or others provide it at a better price?*

■ *What do the users of this service want?*

■ *What is in the best interest of pupils and parents?*

■ *How does the school ensure it receives the most economic, efficient and effective service from those who provide services to pupils and staff?*

You will need to determine whether the school manages its decision-making and assesses the impact on standards of its spending and other decisions in ways that reflect the best value framework. You will need to find out how it balances *costs* (in terms of economy and efficiency) and *effectiveness* (in terms of the performance of the school and the quality of what it provides). This has implications for how you gather and test the evidence from the whole of the inspection, for example your analysis of performance in section 2 and your evaluation of school provision in sections 3 and 4 of the *Evaluation Schedule*.

It is not, however, for inspectors to judge whether best value is being positively achieved; such a judgement is a matter for local accountability. What is required of inspectors is to make information available to parents and other local people about whether the school is applying the best value principle effectively and for them to come to a view about whether best value is being achieved.

Some schools will be more familiar with the principles of best value than others, although some of the elements, such as consultation and comparison, are commonplace in well-managed schools. Schools have been familiar with the value-for-money judgements made by inspectors for years. Best value reflects an attitude to management. You should explore the principles with the school as part of your evaluation of standards, the curriculum, and partnership with parents and management. Best value can be seen as a theme that runs across the different strands of inspection or school evaluation.

Bear in mind that working to these principles is an *expectation* of schools, not a *requirement* – as it is with local authorities. All inspection reports should indicate, however, the extent to which the work of the school reflects best value principles, summarising areas of strength and weakness. Whatever references are made in other areas of the report, your evaluation should be summarised in the leadership and management section.

If, on the evidence of the inspection, the performance of the school is not high enough, you are required to highlight your concerns in the report. These may include the extent to which the school does or does not apply best value principles effectively. These concerns must be set out in the section WHAT SHOULD THE SCHOOL DO TO IMPROVE FURTHER? and in the summary report. These concerns will be reflected in the inspection team's judgement about the school's capacity for improvement and its overall effectiveness, especially the summative judgement about whether the school is underachieving; has serious weaknesses in one or more areas; or is failing, or likely to fail, to give its pupils an acceptable standard of education and therefore requires special measures.

BEST VALUE AND AUDIT

A feature of good school management is the use made of performance review to evaluate how well it is doing and to identify what action is needed to secure improvement. A key task of inspection is to evaluate the school's financial planning, and how it links its strategic use of resources, including specific grants and additional funding, with educational priorities. Many of these areas are covered in financial audit and you will need to make full use of the audit reports in coming to judgements about *costs* and *effectiveness* within the best value framework.

Audit and inspection are complementary processes. The following table identifies key common areas, based on the guidance on schemes of delegation under Fair Funding arrangements.[8] You will need to consider them in the light of evidence from inspection (including budget statements), taking full account of the school's most recent audit. The suggested format will help you organise the evidence and focus your judgements.

---

[8]   See guidance issued by the Secretary of State under schedule 14 of the School Standards and Framework Act 1998.

Questions for audit	Areas for audit/inspection[9]	Questions for inspection
The focus of auditors will be on whether the governing body and the school:		*Inspectors will need to evaluate whether the governing body and school:*
• have set out clear delegation arrangements	**Delegation of powers to the headteacher**	• use delegation wisely
• maintain up-to-date inventories	**Control of assets**	• keep track of its resources
• have a register which is regularly updated and available for scrutiny	**Register of business interests**	• have a register available and whether its contents reveal any significant issues that require following up by others
• have a scheme to cover these arrangements which is used effectively within the best value framework	**Purchasing, tendering and contracting requirements**	• use these arrangements effectively and within the best value framework
• use buy-back services which fall within the scheme of delegation	**Buy-back of services from the LEA or elsewhere**	• effectively use support and other services purchased from the LEA or elsewhere
• regularly and properly have audits carried out	**Audits**	• have acted upon the recommendations to good effect
• submit the budget plan on time and accurately	**Budget plans**	• reflect in the budget plan the priorities set out in the school development plan; if not, why not?
• engage in any irregular spending and/or spending outside the scheme of delegation	**Spending for the purposes of the school**	• spend to reflect the school's purposes and identified priorities for improvement
• have arrangements for ensuring earmarked funds are used for their designated purposes	**Central funds and earmarking funds for designated purposes**	• monitor and evaluate their spending decisions within a best value framework • use earmarked funds only for their designated purposes
• undertake capital spending within regulations	**Capital spending**	• use capital spending appropriately and in line with priorities in the school development plan • monitor and evaluate capital spending decisions within a best value framework

---

[9] See guidance issued by the Secretary of State under schedule 14 of the School Standards and Framework Act 1998.

Questions for audit	Areas for audit/inspection	Questions for inspection
The focus of auditors will be on whether the governing body and the school:		*Inspectors will need to evaluate whether the governing body and school:*
• use their borrowing powers within the scheme of delegation	**Borrowing by schools**	• use borrowing wisely and in line with priorities set out in the school development plan
• ensure any income accrues to the budget • ensure that any cross-subsidy, for example from community or other use of facilities, has no net cost to the school's budget	**Income**	• ensure that arrangements for letting the building for community use benefit the school educationally and are in line with priorities set out in the school development plan
• have a plan for the use of budget surpluses	**Budget surpluses**	• plan to use budget surpluses wisely and in line with priorities set out in the school development plan
• have a justifiable deficit budget, that is licensed by the LEA and linked to an agreed plan for retrieving the budget deficit	**Budget deficits**	• have a deficit budget due to inefficient spending or for other reasons • have a plan for retrieving the deficit which is educationally justifiable and in line with priorities set out in the school development plan
• have a statement setting out what steps are to be taken to ensure best value, and whether the school's management and use of resources adhere to the declared intentions	**Best value**	• apply best value principles effectively in their management and use of resources

Evaluation of best value and financial management should be informed by the items in the right-hand column, although it may not be possible to investigate all of them rigorously.

USE OF PERFORMANCE INDICATORS

You will need to make full use of a range of performance indicators to judge whether the school is applying the best value framework consistently and effectively in its financial planning and management of resources. These indicators will be helpful if set alongside the school's own analysis of its performance (including any value-added analysis undertaken) and the school's account of the management decisions taken by governors, the headteacher and staff about the use of resources.

ANNEX 2

SCHOOLS REQUIRING SPECIAL MEASURES, SCHOOLS WITH SERIOUS WEAKNESSES, AND UNDERACHIEVING SCHOOLS

On every inspection, as a team, you must consider whether the school is failing, or likely to fail, to give its pupils an acceptable standard of education, and therefore requires special measures.

If you judge that the school is providing an acceptable standard of education, the next step is to consider whether it nevertheless has serious weaknesses.

You also need to consider, whether the school, though not identified as having serious weaknesses, is judged to be underachieving.

These judgements must be reported using the prescribed wording, and specific procedures must be followed.

BACKGROUND

The School Inspections Act 1996 (the 1996 Act) states that: 'Special measures are required to be taken in relation to a school if the school is failing or likely to fail to give its pupils an acceptable standard of education' (section 13(9)).

Towards the end of an inspection, as a team, you must consider whether the school is failing, or likely to fail, to give its pupils an acceptable standard of education (Framework, paragraph 33). If you reach this view, and HMCI agrees, then special measures will be required.

If you reach the view that the school is providing its pupils with an acceptable standard of education, you should then and only then consider whether it nevertheless has serious weaknesses.

JUDGING THAT A SCHOOL REQUIRES SPECIAL MEASURES

The possibility that a school may be failing or likely to fail to give its pupils an acceptable standard of education should be considered initially during the pre-inspection analysis of data, indicators and other evidence about the school's performance.

It is uncomfortable coming to a judgement that a school is failing or likely to fail, but it is one which you must not shirk. You must not take the easier course represented by the judgement that the school has serious weaknesses if the evidence points to the conclusion that the school is not providing an acceptable standard of education.

Factors to consider

One feature alone is unlikely to result in a judgement that a school requires special measures, but where you find low standards and poor learning, risk to pupils or the likelihood of a breakdown of discipline, the school will normally require special measures.

The following questions are a guide to the judgement that a school requires special measures.

a.   Education standards achieved:

i.   Is there low achievement in the subjects of the curriculum by the majority of pupils or consistently among particular groups of pupils?   Yes/No

ii.   Is there poor learning and progress in the subjects of the curriculum by the majority of pupils or consistently among particular groups of pupils?   Yes/No

iii.   Are there poor examination results?   Yes/No

iv.   Are the National Curriculum assessment and other accredited results poor?   Yes/No

v.   Is there regular disruptive behaviour?   Yes/No

vi.   Is there a breakdown of discipline?   Yes/No

vii.   Are there high levels of exclusions?   Yes/No

viii. Are there significant levels of racial tension or harassment?   Yes/No

ix.   Is there poor attendance by a substantial proportion of pupils?   Yes/No

x.   Is there poor attendance by particular groups of pupils?   Yes/No

xi.   Is there a high level of truancy?   Yes/No

b.   Quality of education provided:

i.   Is there a high proportion of unsatisfactory teaching?   Yes/No

ii.   Are there low expectations of pupils?   Yes/No

iii.   Is there failure to implement the National Curriculum?   Yes/No

iv.   Is there poor provision for pupils' spiritual, moral, social and cultural development?   Yes/No

v.   Are pupils at physical or emotional risk from other pupils or adults in the school?   Yes/No

vi.   Are there abrasive and confrontational relationships between staff and pupils?   Yes/No

c.   The leadership and management of the school:

i.   Is the headteacher and/or the senior management team and/or the governors ineffective?   Yes/No

ii.   Is there significant loss of confidence in the headteacher by the staff and/or the parents and/or the governors?   Yes/No

iii.   Is there demoralisation and disenchantment amongst staff?   Yes/No

iv.   Are there high levels of staff turnover or absence?   Yes/No

v.   Is there poor management?   Yes/No

vi.   Is inefficient use made of the resources available to the school, including finance?   Yes/No

vii.   Does the school apply principles of best value in its use of resources?   Yes/No

You may also find the following forms useful in arriving at decisions:

EDUCATIONAL STANDARDS ACHIEVED	serious concern	some concern	no concern
Achievement in:			
English/communication – including literacy			
Mathematics – including numeracy			
Science			
Design and technology			
Information technology			
History			
Geography			
Modern foreign languages			
Music			
Art			
PE			
In NC subjects or curriculum overall			
Religious education – special schools only			
PSHE			
Post-16 provision			
Other curricular provision			
National test/examination results			
Behaviour			
Level of exclusions			
Level of racial tension or harassment			
Attendance			
Truancy			

QUALITY OF EDUCATION PROVIDED	serious concern	some concern	no concern
Teaching			
Expectations of pupils			
Implementation of the National Curriculum			
Provision for pupils' SMSC development			
Pupils at physical/emotional risk from other pupils			
Pupils at physical/emotional risk from adults			
Relationships between staff and pupils			
LEADERSHIP AND MANAGEMENT OF THE SCHOOL Effectiveness of headteacher			
Effectiveness of other senior managers			
Effectiveness of the governors			
Confidence in the headteacher by staff			
Confidence in the headteacher by parents			
Confidence in the headteacher by governors			
Demoralisation and disenchantment among staff			
Level of staff turnover/absence			
Management/use made of available resources			
Principles of best value applied by the school			
School improvement since last inspection			
Ability to secure necessary improvements			

A school will be likely to fail if it:

- is close to the point where it would be judged to be failing;

- is declining rapidly in one or a number of important areas;

- is in decline and this is not being checked by the senior managers and appropriate authority;

- is in a precarious state where the management is ineffective and therefore the quality of education is likely to decline;

- has many weaknesses and had made insufficient progress since the last inspection.

Procedures to be followed

If the accumulating evidence suggests that the school may require special measures, you can get further guidance during office hours from the School Improvement Division in OFSTED (telephone 020 7421 6594). If, as a team, you reach the judgement that the school is failing or likely to fail, and therefore requires special measures, the registered inspector must:

- inform the School Improvement Division in OFSTED before the school is told of the judgement;

- before leaving the school at the end of the inspection, tell the headteacher orally either that in the view of the inspection team there are serious deficiencies and that the team is considering whether the school is failing, or likely to fail, to give its pupils an acceptable standard of education, or that the inspection team has reached a corporate judgement that the school is failing or likely to fail to give its pupils an acceptable standard of education;

- when giving oral reports to the senior management team and the appropriate authority, state that the corporate judgement of the inspection team is that the school is failing, or likely to fail, to give its pupils an acceptable standard of education. The following form of words could be used:

    I am of the opinion that special measures are required in relation to this school because it is failing (or likely to fail) to give its pupils an acceptable standard of education. In accordance with section 13(2) of the School Inspections Act 1996 I shall send a draft report to HMCI and will await his judgement on whether he agrees or not that the school requires special measures.

- explain that submission of the draft report to OFSTED may delay the issue of the report to the appropriate authority. The maximum delay is three months from the date when the report was due;

- use *Form 1* at the end of this section to inform the School Improvement Division in OFSTED of the team's decision;

- submit to OFSTED, but not to the school, the draft report and any other papers that are required as quickly as possible and by the agreed date, and always within five weeks of the end of the inspection.

What happens next?

HMI will consider the evidence and may visit the school before recommending to HMCI whether or not to agree that the school requires special measures. Whenever possible, if a visit is to take place, it will be within three working weeks of the inspection. The purpose of the visit will be to confirm or otherwise that special measures are required; HMI will not be re-inspecting the school.

If you are the registered inspector, you must ensure that all the evidence collected during the inspection is available for scrutiny by HMCI. It is probable that, on behalf of HMCI, the School Improvement Division will ask you to provide:

■ the school prospectus;

■ a plan of the school and a map showing its location;

■ timetables and a copy of any key that is necessary to be able to interpret the timetables;

■ the draft report and summary;

■ the completed *Record of Corporate Judgements* (including JRF grades), all completed *Inspection Notebooks* (including subject JRF grades), and *Evidence Forms*;

■ *Forms S1–S4*;

■ a note of the main issues raised at the parents' meeting and in the parents' questionnaire responses.

When HMI have scrutinised the evidence and, in some cases, visited the school, they report to HMCI. He will decide whether or not he agrees with the team's opinion and will tell you of his decision.

If HMCI agrees with the judgement that the school is failing or likely to fail, the following form of words should be used in the summary report:

> *In accordance with section 13(7) of the School Inspections Act 1996 I am of the opinion, and HMCI agrees, that special measures are required in relation to this school.*

If HMCI does not agree, the reasons will be explained and you will be given the opportunity to discuss HMCI's decision. Three options are open to you:

■ accept HMCI's decision and amend the report by removing the opinion that the school requires special measures, and then issue the report;

■ decide to issue the report without amendment. Special measures will not apply and you must then use the following form of words in the main findings of the report and in the summary:

> *In accordance with section 13(7) of the School Inspection Act 1996, I am of the opinion, but HMCI disagrees, that special measures are required in relation to this school.*

■ prepare further drafts for HMCI to consider, incorporating the opinion that the school is failing, or likely to fail. If HMCI still disagrees after considering subsequent drafts, you may decide to issue the report and summary without further amendment, but must state that HMCI disagrees with you using the form of words above. The report and summary must be substantially the same as the latest drafts sent to HMCI. Special measures will not apply.

JUDGING THAT A SCHOOL HAS SERIOUS WEAKNESSES

Factors to consider

If, as a team, you reach the view that the school is giving an acceptable standard of education, you should then consider whether or not it nevertheless has serious weaknesses in one or more areas of its work. In doing so, you should refer to the same characteristics as those you considered when deciding whether or not the school is giving an acceptable standard of education. You should make your judgements in the light of the findings as a whole, but should normally view the following weaknesses as significant:

- low standards of achievement and/or unsatisfactory learning and progress made, particularly in the core subjects;

- unsatisfactory teaching in about one in eight lessons;

- ineffective leadership and/or management.

Procedures to be followed

The registered inspector should tell the headteacher at the end of the inspection either that the team's view is that there are deficiencies and that it is considering whether the school has serious weaknesses, or that it has reached the judgement that the school has serious weaknesses. You must tell the School Improvement Division in OFSTED of your decision by telephone (020 7421 6594) before you tell the school, and subsequently send OFSTED the attached *Form 2*.

You should use a very clear form of words in the summary report. The words 'This school has serious weaknesses' must be included.

A copy of the final report should be sent to the School Improvement Division at the same time as it is sent to the school.

For further information and guidance about special measures or serious weaknesses, contact:

School Improvement Division
OFSTED
Alexandra House
33 Kingsway
London WC2B 6SE

Telephone: 020 7421 6594

JUDGING THAT A SCHOOL IS UNDERACHIEVING

A judgement about whether a school is underachieving will be made, in appropriate circumstances, as part of both SHORT and FULL INSPECTIONS.

Factors to consider

The judgement should be made by considering:

- the effectiveness of the school;
- improvement since the last inspection;
- the performance of the school in comparison with schools in similar contexts.

It should be made on the basis of **performance data** and **inspection judgements** taken together.

Performance data

The performance data should include the following as applied to the highest Key Stage in the school, up to 16:

- the school's results, compared with all schools nationally;
- the school's results, compared with schools in similar contexts, using QCA benchmarks;
- whether the school's average NC levels are improving over time, compared to the trend in national average NC levels.

For the majority of schools, the like-school comparison will be based on QCA free school meal bandings, as before.

You should consider the grade codes for national comparison and like-school comparisons, given in the *PICSI report*:

A* –   very high in comparison with national average/average for similar schools

A   –   well above the national average/average for similar schools

B   –   above the national average/average for similar schools

C   –   average (in line with) the national average/average for similar schools

D   –   below the national average/average for similar schools

E   –   well below the national average/average for similar schools

E* –   very low in comparison with the national average/average for similar schools.

The performance data could, therefore, indicate elements of underachievement. Possible underachievement would be identified as part of the *Pre-Inspection Commentary* and provide a focus for the inspection. For example, for cases such as:

Grade for national comparison	Grade for comparison with schools in similar contexts	Trends in results
A*, A, B	D	Slower than national trends *or* no significant change over time
C	D/E	Slower than national trend
		No significant change over time

In addition, for sixth forms, the most significant indication of underachievement is in the value-added figure from GCSE to GCE Advanced level or GNVQ, and the extent to which it is significantly below the national average figure.

Inspection judgements

Evidence for underachievement found during the inspection will focus largely on aspects of teaching, learning, leadership and management, in conjunction with the hypotheses suggested by the data, as above. Significant pointers might be:

Teaching and learning

- where the percentage of good or better teaching is low;

- where the capacity of the teaching to challenge and inspire pupils is judged unsatisfactory, especially for higher-attaining pupils and other specific groups of pupils such as pupils with special educational needs or for whom English is an additional language, even if the teaching overall is satisfactory;

- where the methods used to enable all pupils to learn effectively are judged unsatisfactory, although the teaching is judged satisfactory overall;

- where the pupils' application of intellectual, physical or creative effort is judged unsatisfactory, although pupils' learning is judged satisfactory overall;

- where the extent to which pupils show interest in their work, concentrate and think and learn for themselves is judged unsatisfactory, although pupils' learning is judged satisfactory overall.

Leadership and management

- where the monitoring, evaluation and development of teaching is judged unsatisfactory;

- where the shared commitment to improvement and the capacity to succeed are judged unsatisfactory;

- where the school's targets are not appropriate and/or progress towards meeting them is unsatisfactory.

School improvement

- where the judgement that the school has improved since the last inspection is barely satisfactory, overall, with specific and identifiable reservations based on the previous report and other sources of evidence.

The **overall judgement** that a school is underachieving would be based on:

- the performance data, which show the school's results are not as good as they could be;

- evidence that results are not improving sufficiently but not to the extent of being a serious weakness;

- significant concerns about aspects of **teaching, learning, leadership and management**, although these concerns are not acute enough to merit a judgement of serious weaknesses overall.

Procedures to be followed

The registered inspector should tell the headteacher at the end of the inspection either that the team's view is that it is considering whether the school is underachieving, or that it has reached the judgement that the school is underachieving. You must tell the School Improvement Division in OFSTED of your decision by telephone (020 7421 6594) before you tell the school, and subsequently send OFSTED the attached *Form 2*. You should use words 'This school is underachieving' in the summary report. A copy of the final report should be sent to the School Improvement Division at the same time as it is sent to the school.

For further information and guidance about underachieving schools, contact:

School Improvement Division
OFSTED
Alexandra House
33 Kingsway
London WC2B 6SE

Telephone: 020 7421 6594

RECOMMENDATION FOR SPECIAL MEASURES

This form must be used by **all** lead inspectors to confirm the judgement that the school requires special measures. **Immediately the school has been informed of the decision, this form must be sent to:**

Head of the School Improvement Division
OFSTED
Alexandra House
Room 802
33 Kingsway
London WC2B 6SE

Inspection Number ....

Date of inspection ..../.........../...........

School name ....

Village/town ....

Status ....

Local Education Authority ....

Name of lead inspector ....
[RgI] [AI] [HMI] (delete as appropriate)

Date when report and summary are due ..../.........../...........

I am of the opinion that special measures are required in relation to this school, since it is failing/likely to fail to give its pupils an acceptable standard of education. The reasons for this opinion are:

1

2

3

4

(Please continue on separate sheet if necessary.)

I will send you drafts of the report and the summary by ..../.........../...........

I confirm that I will report in these terms to the senior management team of the school and to the governors.

Signed...

Name (please print).. Date ..../.........../..........

Telephone number...

Address...

FORM 2

CONFIRMATION OF SERIOUS WEAKNESSES *OR* THAT THE SCHOOL IS UNDERACHIEVING

This form must be used by **all** lead inspectors to confirm the judgement that the school has serious weaknesses **or** is underachieving. **Immediately the school has been informed of the decision, this form must be sent to:**

Head of the School Improvement Division
OFSTED
Alexandra House
Room 802
33 Kingsway
London WC2B 6SE

Date of inspection ..../........../..........

Date when report and summary are due ..../........../..........

I will send you the final report and the summary by ..../........../..........

School name ....

Village/town ....

Status ....

Local Education Authority ....

Name of lead inspector ....
[RgI] [AI] [HMI] (delete as appropriate)

Delete as appropriate:

I am of the opinion that this school is giving its pupils an acceptable standard of education, but it is a school with serious weaknesses. The reasons for this opinion are:

or

I am of the opinion that this school is underachieving. The reasons for this opinion are:

1

2

3

4

(Please continue on separate sheet if necessary.)

I confirm that I will report in these terms to the senior management team of the school and to the governors.

Signed...

Name (please print)... Date ..../........../..........

Telephone number...

Address...

ANNEX 3

COMPLETING THE RECORD OF INSPECTION EVIDENCE

(A) COMPLETING THE *PRE-INSPECTION COMMENTARY*

What to include

The essential features of the *Pre-Inspection Commentary* are:

■ your preliminary views of the school in all areas of the *Evaluation Schedule*;

■ initial hypotheses, to be tested during the inspection, in each of these areas.

Using the *Pre-Inspection Commentary*

The evidence on which you base your views and hypotheses will come mainly from three sources, and you might find it helpful to structure your *Pre-Inspection Commentary* using these three areas. They are:

■ factual information from the *PICSI report* and other sources, such as *Forms S1* and *S2*;

■ the school's previous inspection report;

■ qualitative information you gain from *Forms S3* and *S4* and your visit to the school.

You should complete the *Pre-Inspection Commentary* in two stages. You will be able to begin writing the commentary when you have received the *PICSI report* and the completed inspection forms. The data contained in the *PICSI report* and *Forms S1* and *S2* will enable you to analyse the school's achievements in national tests. The headteacher's responses on *Forms S3* and *S4* will give you a picture of the school's own view of itself. You will then have sufficient knowledge of the school to put together a set of questions to ask the headteacher on the preliminary visit.

The information you obtain from the preliminary visit will enable you to complete the *Pre-Inspection Commentary* so that all team members have a clear picture of the school, in all areas of the *Evaluation Schedule*, before the inspection begins.

At the end of each section of the commentary you should include one or two key hypotheses for the inspection team to test out. Try to avoid long lists of hypotheses and focus on the 'big issues'. There is no need to include the reporting requirements or the criteria from the *Evaluation Schedule* because you will use these as a matter of course to evaluate the evidence in all inspections. What is needed is a small number of issues, which are drawn clearly from the evidence so far available and which relate specifically to the school being inspected.

In most cases these hypotheses will need to be followed up by all inspectors, and in a SHORT INSPECTION this will certainly be the case. In a FULL INSPECTION, individual team members may need to focus on particular issues and report back to the team at a suitable team meeting. You may find it helpful to indicate in the *Pre-Inspection Commentary* how an issue will be followed up, and by whom.

Style of writing

The *Pre-Inspection Commentary* needs to be concise and to the point. You will most likely write in continuous prose in short paragraphs. You should not rehearse all the evidence you have considered, which is contained in the *PICSI*, inspection forms and the school's documentation. Your commentary should contain your views, so far, of what you have seen and discussed. The hypotheses should also be brief and to the point.

Extract from **Pre-Inspection Commentary** *partially completed before the preliminary visit to the school*

Example before the school visit

2 How high are standards?	Interpretation of the school's results

Pre-inspection analysis of attainment:

Evaluation drawing on performance data, indicating Key Stages or groups of pupils, where relevant

Previous report:

- *At the time of the last inspection pupils entered the school with attainment levels at the national average.*

- *Standards at the end of KS3 were well above average in EN and MA but were in line in SC.*

- *At the end of KS4 GCSE results then showed continuing strong performance in EN and MA, with SC improving and above the national average. DR was found to be exceptionally good and standards in EN, MA, AR and HI were high. All other subjects were achieving results in line with the national average, with only GG below.*

- *Boys achieved better results than boys nationally, but girls were around the national average for girls, and only slightly ahead of the boys. Overall, the school performed at about the national average at GCSE.*

- *Key issues in the report were to improve the performance and progress of higher-attaining pupils, and to improve standards in GG.*

PICSI report:

KS3: *Last year the school's NC test results show that pupils are about one half of a level above the national average: this is significant and puts the school in the A (well above) category. There has been a similar pattern over the last three years. However, compared with similar schools, the school is graded only C (average). Last year's results for EN, MA and SC are consistent, with EN slightly weaker than MA, an improvement on the previous year when EN results were below national averages by half a level, and MA well above. MA also does better than average in comparison with similar schools (B), whereas EN and SC are graded C (average). Last year boys attained standards relatively higher than girls when compared with the results of boys and girls nationally (+0.61 as against +0.32 levels). This reversed the position at the time of the last inspection (+0.31 as against +0.56 levels). Boys have now overtaken girls to achieve higher standards overall at the end of KS3 in core subjects, suggesting that the attainment of boys is a possible strength of the school.*

KS4: *All the data point to high standards, well above the national average. A steady increase of five A*–C grades has been achieved from 42 to 68 per cent over four years, averaging 6 per cent a year, with surges from year to year. The percentage of A*–G grades has increased more erratically, but from 90 to 98 per cent. In relation to points scores, the school is well above average (A) for both boys and girls, with last year's results for girls putting them in A*. Differences in attainment between boys and girls reflect the national pattern, with girls further ahead. In subjects last year DR, EN and MA all performed significantly above the national average. However, AR, GG and MFL all performed worse.*

*Extract from the same **Pre-Inspection Commentary** showing the section written after the preliminary visit, and including the main issues for exploration during the inspection*

Example after the school visit

| 2   How high are standards? | Interpretation of the school's results |

Pre-inspection analysis of attainment:

Evaluation drawing on performance data, indicating Key Stages or groups of pupils, where relevant

Pre-inspection visit:

HT has instituted a comprehensive analysis of performance data by subject, Key Stage, gender, ethnic group and teaching group. School is gaining a precise fix on value added by recent initiatives. For example, HT spoke confidently about the switch in boy/girl performance and further increases in standards for higher-attainers. EN results in the previous year affected by marking difficulties nationally that year, but aware that EN TA and NC test results varied unduly, also boy/girl ratio was 2:1. HT very satisfied with last year's results. Keen to assert that five A*–C pass rates vary in accordance with the numbers of SEN pupils in the year group. From LEA data on site it was clear that the school achieves the highest points score of all its schools, and the highest percentage of A* and A grades.

HT and senior managers spoke enthusiastically about the school's improvement project focusing on higher-attaining pupils, which is viewed as attracting the wider range of applications for admission and is very popular with parents. This is reflected in the returns in the parents' questionnaire, where high standards are stated as a recent magnet by many. The down side is some failure to identify relatively weaker subjects sufficiently closely, for example GG. Penetrating analyses of strengths in MA, DR, AR and HI seen in departmental reviews, but again less sharp on weaker subjects such as SC, and to some extent KS3 EN. HT of the view that difficulties with GG staffing have affected standards, but recent appointments already making a difference, particularly in KS4.

Initial hypotheses and areas for exploration:

1. *Is the school improvement project on higher-attainers continuing to improve standards in all subjects?*

2. *How does this impact on average, lower-attaining and SEN pupils?*

3. *How has the school responded to the key issues in the previous inspection report: to improve the performance and progress of the higher-attainers, and to improve standards in GG?*

(B) COMPLETING THE *EVIDENCE FORM*

What to include

The *Evidence Form* is structured so that the same form can be used to record inspection evidence in four areas:

- **lesson observations** (coded **L**), including the observation of small groups or individual tuition;

- **analysis of pupils' work** (coded **A**), which might be undertaken independently of the pupils, or with the pupils present, to gain further insights into standards;

- **discussions** (coded **D**) with pupils, staff, governors and others;

- **any other evidence** (coded **O**), including observations of assemblies, registration periods, breaktimes, lunchtimes, arrival and departure from school and extra-curricular activities, and commentary on the school's documentation.

In writing each *Evidence Form*, you will need to complete the following parts:

- the **context** in which the form has been completed;

- the **evidence** you wish to record;

- when used for lesson observations, and optionally in other cases, **grades** for: teaching; learning; attainment; and attitudes and values;

- the **coding** boxes at the top.

Using the *Evidence Form*

Evidence Forms (EFs) are the key records of firsthand inspection evidence and your judgements on the basis of that evidence. You will need to refer to them when you identify strengths and weaknesses in your *Inspection Notebook*. They are also the source of illustrations for the inspection report.

When OFSTED's Inspection Quality Division monitors an inspection, the monitoring HMI may wish to look at the quality of evidence, judgement and grades recorded on *Evidence Forms*.

The context box

In the **context box**, put enough to describe the situation being recorded. If you are using the *EF* to record a discussion, say whom it is with and what it is about. If the *EF* is for a lesson or other observation, briefly describe what the teacher and pupils are doing so that someone else could visualise the situation you observed. If you are recording your analysis of pupils' work, include sufficient detail to identify the work with the relevant subject or subjects and year or Key Stage.

Example of a context box for a lesson observation

Context:

Food technology lesson (Y8). Focus of the lesson is tasting products. Started with whole class discussion about appearance, taste and texture of products and importance of packaging. Pupils then tasted the different products and recorded their observations.

The evidence box

In the **evidence box** you should record the evidence you have collected and your judgements on the basis of that evidence. Each *EF* should contain:

■ sufficient **evidence** to support the judgement(s) you make, in that anyone reading the evidence would be very likely to come to the same judgement;

Example of a lesson observation – recording evidence

Evidence:

Most pupils have a good understanding of the use of brackets in calculations and how they help to avoid errors. Their spatial sense is very good. Level of work generally at Level 5 or 6 – for about three-quarters of the class. Some are skilled at giving a rough estimate as an answer, before using the calculator, even when using square roots. Attainment above average.

Y8 mathematics lesson   **Attainment – Grade 3**

■ a strong **focus on strengths and weaknesses**, and what makes them strengths and weaknesses, with less emphasis on that which is satisfactory but has no major positive or negative features;

Example of a lesson observation – recording strengths and weaknesses

Evidence:

Tasks set as a puzzle, geometrically done using pencil and compasses, which pupils tackled very well. Teacher good at allowing hypotheses without agreeing or disagreeing until time for the group to make its decision (S). Too long spent without hint that the 'results' are hypotheses only at this stage, and some opportunities missed for pupils to contribute explanations of why some of these work and others do not (W). Class very well managed, with supportive relationships and effective match of task to pupils' prior learning, reflecting good planning, careful resourcing and effective use of time (S).

Y9 mathematics lesson   **Teaching and learning – Grade 3**

■ **illustrations** which can be drawn on by you or other inspectors when writing text for the report, particularly of strengths and weaknesses;

Example of a lesson observation – recording illustrations

Evidence:

Pupils showed very good understanding when exploring the techniques of rhetoric and persuasion – spoken and written – when constructing a pamphlet on bullying for a local primary school. Theory and practice, abstract and concrete, understood, with a quick realisation of the issues, the importance of evidence and of the syntactical features of persuasive writing and its use. Clear progress evident, with real gains in vocabulary for many.

Y10 English lesson   **Learning – Grade 2**

■ **judgements** made on the basis of the evidence and, in the case of lesson observations, summary judgements on teaching and learning; attainment; attitudes and behaviour;

Example of a lesson observation – recording judgements

Evidence:

Clear introduction to the prevalence of drink in advertisements. Good pace to the positive, demanding, challenging teaching, with a whole class focus to direct attention to a variety of synonyms for 'sober'. Good short-term demands on vocabulary, with quickfire Q and A and pressure on response times, promoting energetic mental vitality. No room for passengers here, everyone kept up to scratch. Pace excellent, quickening as the lesson developed. Sharp focus on alcohol as part of the culture of youth, using effective literary references. Managed pupil group discussions on legal implications very sensitively and succeeded in engaging all. No time for summing up, however.

Y10 PSE lesson   **Teaching – Grade 2**

■ **explanations** that justify why things are as they are.

Example of a lesson observation – recording explanations

Evidence:

Pupils were not well challenged by this lesson because the teacher's expectations were very low for the level of discussion accepted and for the conduct of the role-play on the five pillars of Islam. The lesson lacked structure and was not well planned, so that pupils were unclear as to how the work linked to their previous learning and what was expected of them. The attempt at evaluation following the role-play was therefore doomed to failure, as the teacher did not demonstrate the necessary subject knowledge, with the effect that pupils' learning was not extended, and they lost interest and became restless.

Y9 RE lesson   **Teaching – Grade 6**

You may wish additionally to use part of this space to record, for example the way pupils with special educational needs learn, or how pupils with English as an additional language are supported by the use of information and communications technology (ICT) in all subjects. This focused approach is most effective when used consistently by all members of the inspection team in every lesson observation.

The grade boxes

When you enter **grades** at the foot of the form, make sure they match the judgements in the text above about teaching and learning, attainment, and pupils' attitudes and behaviour. You should always grade lesson observations. You may find it helpful to grade *EF*s that record your analysis of pupils' work, and any *EF*s coded 0 in which there is an element of teaching, such as in an assembly or in some extra-curricular activities.

In **lesson observations** you must always grade **teaching, learning,** and pupils' **attitudes and behaviour.** In most cases you will use Grades 1–7 but you may need to use 0 if there is too little evidence to make a secure judgement. On very rare occasions, you may need to use 8 to indicate that it is not appropriate to enter a grade. Wherever possible, you should enter a grade for attainment. If you feel you do not have the expertise to make a judgement about attainment, for example if you are a lay inspector, it is acceptable to leave the attainment grade blank.

You should try to use the full range of grades. So, for example, if pupils' learning in a lesson is exemplary and you cannot see how it could be improved, award a Grade 1 and make sure that the text on the *EF* supports this grade.

Filling in the coded boxes at the top of the form

Every time you write an *EF* you need to code, where possible, the sections at the top of the form. The diagram shows what is needed. Further details are provided on the CD-ROM accompanying this *Handbook*.

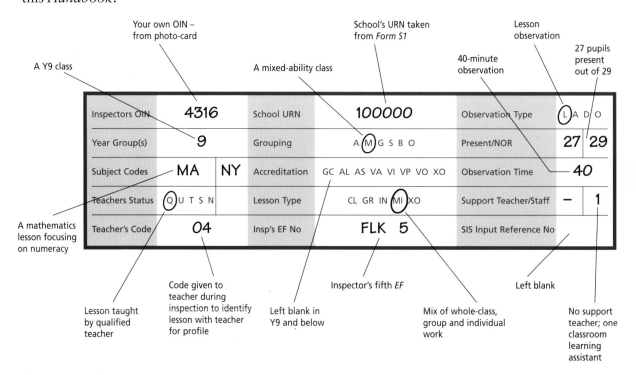

Style of writing

There is no prescribed format for completion of *EF*s. Effective writing could be in continuous prose or in note form; it could list strengths and weaknesses separately or cover the same ground within a single piece of text. What matters is that the *EF* communicates to others the essential features of what has been seen or discussed.

In **lesson observations,** the pieces of evidence you obtain for teaching and learning are often inextricably linked. When you write the *EF* you should integrate these two areas whenever you can. You may wish to note particular points in each area that help you reach the two separate grades needed. If the grades for teaching and learning are different, for example if the teacher did all he or she could but other factors meant that pupils' learning was not graded as highly, you need to explain why they are different.

Example of a lesson observation – recording differences in judgements

Evidence:

Weaknesses in teaching techniques, e.g., teacher questioned the class when half the class had their backs to her and were not involved in the Q and A. Similarly not all could see the OHTs, as part shown on the screen, part on the wall. Quite lively when talking about dissolving milk, but lost on many pupils because of the layout of the room, and the teacher talked while pupils intent on drawing their diagrams. Slow pace, but picked up later. Teacher at no time checked pupils' understanding, but it was clear from their output that they knew what to do and could explain it in terms of movement of particles. They coped well with the solubility curve and demonstrated good graphical skills by the end of the lesson.

Y9 science lesson   **Teaching – Grade 5; Learning – Grade 4**

In the **analysis of pupils' work** you should primarily use the *EF* to give a clear picture of pupils' attainment. You can use the *EF* to record the attainment of different groups of pupils and your exploration of differences in the standards achieved by pupils of different gender or ethnic background. You should also try, where you can, to bring out any evidence about teaching, pupils' learning and their attitudes.

Example of recording the analysis of pupils' work

Context:

Extract from the analysis of Y11 work in English

Evidence:

Very high standards in powerful imaginative prose, with critical reflection on the methods and purposes behind the writing. The sample also suggests a mature blend of criticism linked to creative practice of an unusually high standard.

Good range of writing, covering narrative, poetry, stories, letters, drama scripts for video role-play and newspaper articles. Unusually talented analyses of the stylistic features of tabloid journalism alongside carefully argued and penetrative critical essay writing on Macbeth. Most writing in this top set reflects a fluent and confident style which capably relates interpretation and analysis naturally and with ease, whilst including very effective textual references.

Exceptional progress during the GCSE course, with virtually all pupils' work likely to achieve A grades. Pupils' work reflects an eagerness to develop their strengths and learn from the teacher's comments on it. This was true of most of the work seen completed by girls.

Particularly successful and sensitive responses to a challenging range of modern poetry, e.g., Auden, Lockhead, Heaney. Impressive drafting and note-making skills, especially since the mock examinations; as an extension, some very effective spider diagrams, with girls relating text and interpretation well. Very high levels of technical competence in the pupils' letters, diaries and reports completed, for example on 1984, including impressive understanding of 'newspeak'.

Attainment – Grade 1; Learning – Grade 1

When you write about **discussions** with pupils, staff, governors or others, you should record the key points of the discussion, not try to transcribe all of what was said. This is often easier if the discussion takes place using a set of headings designed specifically for that occasion. At the end of the discussions, if there is time, you might find it helpful to go briefly through what you have written to check you have the main points accurately recorded.

Example of a record of a discussion with headteacher on management

Context:

Extract from a record of a discussion with HT about the monitoring of teaching

Evidence:

There has been an established policy of monitoring the quality of teaching through lesson observation for the past five years.

This is conducted on a departmental basis, with HoD observing each teacher in the department once each term, with any new teachers observing HoD and DHoD once each also. Findings inform departmental planning at monthly meetings. Three departments have moved on to informal peer observation of their teaching on a regular basis as time allows: MA, HI, DT. HT is of the view that this is steadily helping to improve standards and correct unevenness identified in the last inspection report in DT.

In addition, as part of the programme of annual monitoring and evaluation through departmental review, HT and DHT conduct lesson observation of two departments each year, using the OFSTED Framework criteria for teaching. Teachers are observed teaching in each Key Stage in lessons to two separate groups of different attainment levels. The observer makes use of an EF and debriefs the teacher fully following the lesson. HT and DHT meet with the whole department for a summary discussion of the findings, and a report is presented to the governing body with HoD present. There has been occasional slippage, but each department will have been reviewed within the next year, with only MFL outstanding. In two cases, GG and PE, this has resulted in extensive provision of additional INSET, and support from the LEA adviser.

The English department has been particularly innovative with its move to joint teaching following peer lesson observation, and has presented a paper to other HoDs on the outcomes, drawing on its significantly improved GCSE results over the past three years and its recent involvement with the QCA literacy work for KS3.

Overall evaluation: SMT and middle managers are developing a very clear picture of the strengths and weaknesses in the quality of teaching in subject departments, and this has helped to rack up standards and reduce inconsistencies in pupils' experiences. The sixth form has as yet remained outside this development and governors are seeking an early report.

(C) COMPLETION OF *INSPECTION NOTEBOOKS*

What to include

On FULL INSPECTIONS and on SHORT INSPECTIONS, where it is used, the *Inspection Notebook* should always include:

- judgements in as many areas of the *Evaluation Schedule* as possible for which you have evidence, expressed as strengths and weaknesses;

- references to the *Evidence Forms* which form the basis for these judgements, and which can be used to illustrate them, if needed, in the inspection report;

- an overall evaluation under each *Evaluation Schedule* heading for which you have evidence.

When you are inspecting a subject or more than one subject during a FULL INSPECTION, your *Notebook* should additionally contain:

- a section on pre-inspection evidence about those subjects, written using the guidance given above for completing the *Pre-Inspection Commentary*;

- a summary of the feedback you intend to give to the co-ordinator for each subject you are inspecting, at or towards the end of the inspection;

- grades for the judgement recording statements in each of the subjects you are responsible for;

- the time you have spent on firsthand inspection in the school.

In a FULL INSPECTION, when you are responsible for writing aspects or subject sections of the report, the *Inspection Notebook* will also contain:

- the draft text of your contributions to the inspection report, usually completed after the final team meeting.

Using the *Inspection Notebook*

Each inspector, including the registered inspector, must complete an *Inspection Notebook* in a FULL INSPECTION, and the completed form will be entered into the inspection software. You may use one in a SHORT INSPECTION if you find it convenient to do so, but its contents will not be entered into the inspection software. It will, however, form part of the evidence base for the inspection.

The *Inspection Notebook* is for you to record your own views and judgements on the evidence you have collected. You should use it after you have reflected on the evidence from a number of sources. For example, after seeing several lessons on the first day of an inspection, you will probably feel you have sufficient evidence about teaching to record your views and make some tentative judgements about the quality of teaching. You should express your views as strengths and weaknesses. There is no need to include extensive commentary on things which are satisfactory. These views would form the basis of your contribution to the inspection team's discussions about teaching at a team meeting. You would be able to illustrate your points by referring back to the evidence on your *Evidence Forms*. For this reason, you will need to include a reference to the source(s) of evidence against each judgement recorded.

You will probably find that, in some areas of the *Evaluation Schedule*, you will be combining evidence from a range of different sources before writing in your *Inspection Notebook*. For example, your views on pupils' behaviour will come from *Evidence Forms* covering lessons, what you have seen outside lessons and discussions with staff and pupils.

In FULL INSPECTIONS, where you are inspecting more than one subject or aspect, you will need to structure your *Notebook* according to the subjects and/or aspects you are responsible for. If you are responsible for inspecting more than one subject, you will need to complete a judgement recording form for each. Your *Notebook* should incorporate the evidence from other team members who may have inspected work in 'your' subjects.

Whether you fill in your *Inspection Notebook* by hand or using a computer, you should treat it as a running commentary, which can be modified and added to as the inspection proceeds.

Towards the end of the inspection, you will need to make an overall evaluation of the evidence you have obtained under each heading in the *Evaluation Schedule*. You will also need to make sure that all the strengths and weaknesses recorded represent your final considered judgements, as these will be entered into the inspection software with the other inspection information.

You will also need to record the source(s) from which you derived each judgement. This will be a reference to one or more *Evidence Forms*, possibly from other inspectors on the team. In a FULL INSPECTION you will need copies of these forms if you are writing a subject or aspect, so that you can refer to them after the inspection has finished.

When an inspection is monitored by OFSTED's Inspection Quality Division, the monitoring HMI may wish to look at the quality of evaluations and judgements contained in *Inspection Notebooks*.

The subject judgement recording form

Towards or at the end of each FULL INSPECTION, you will need to enter grades in each subject inspected for the judgement recording statements at the back of the *Inspection Notebook*. The numbering follows that of the school judgement recording statements in the *Record of Corporate Judgements*. The grades should fall naturally into place from the judgements you have recorded in the earlier pages of the *Inspection Notebook*. If assigning a grade is difficult, it probably indicates that you have not already made or not recorded a clear judgement. In these circumstances you are advised to go back to consider the judgement itself, making use of the strengths and weaknesses you have recorded and, if necessary, referring to *Evidence Forms*.

Style of writing

You use the *Inspection Notebook* to record judgements, summarise your views and point to the evidence on which they are based. It should be written very concisely, therefore. It should consist of:

- single-sentence statements, or the equivalent in note form;
- coded references to *Evidence Forms*, using the code entered in the box at the top of each relevant form.

Example of an extract from a page of an Inspection Notebook

3   How well are pupils or students taught?   Teaching and learning

What is the quality of teaching and what is its impact?

Strengths and weaknesses from the inspection, indicating groups of pupils and Key Stages where relevant, and an overall evaluation.

Sources of evidence:

Strengths:

- *Teaching in design and technology: very effective impact on pupils' understanding and the pace of their learning* — HM 10

- *Secure subject knowledge: especially good in KS4 and in the sixth form in SC, up to date in food technology* — HM 2, 6

- *Very good relationships with pupils through well planned but relaxed management of lessons, e.g., SC, DT* — All EFs

- *Clarity of explanation and objectives, assisting pupils' swift start to work and their understanding* — All EFs

- *High expectations and demands of pupils, particularly sixth formers in SC, MA* — HM 4, 11

- *Very effective small group work, setting sharply focused tasks with challenge and good stimulation, e.g., SC, PSE* — HM 5, 9, 12

Weaknesses:

- *Occasional lack of differentiation, with over-reliance on worksheets and pupils' output, e.g., KS3 DT, some MA KS3* — HM 1, 3, 8

- *Failure to support pupils with SEN in some MA lessons leading to lack of progress and restlessness* — HM 1, 7, 8

Overall evaluation:

Clear strengths of very effective teaching based on comprehensive subject knowledge, good explanation and thoughtful strategies of interaction with pupils, through challenging both individuals and small groups to do of their best in achieving high expectations set. Pupils with SEN sometimes overlooked.

(D) COMPLETION OF THE *RECORD OF CORPORATE JUDGEMENTS*

What to include

The *Record of Corporate Judgements* for your inspection must include:

- corporate judgements of the inspection team in each area of the *Evaluation Schedule*;

- agreed grades for each of the judgement recording statements required in your inspection;

- agreed grades for each of the additional judgement recording statements *P1–P10*;

- agreed grades and, where necessary, reasons for changes of grade, to the similar school comparisons;

- statements and, where necessary, reasons for your decisions about whether the school requires special measures, has serious weaknesses or is underachieving;

- a summary of the extent and range of the inspection evidence.

Using the *Record of Corporate Judgements*

A single *Record of Corporate Judgements (RCJ)* is used in each inspection. It is completed at team meetings towards the end of an inspection and/or at the final team meeting after the inspection. You should use the *Record of Corporate Judgements* to record the team's agreed judgements and point to the evidence on which they are based. When parts of the *RCJ* are completed at an earlier team meeting, the contents of these parts will need to be confirmed at the final team meeting after the inspection. Because, as the registered inspector, you will be managing these meetings, it will be helpful if the actual recording is carried out by another member of the team, leaving you free to focus on the team's judgements.

The order of the pages in the *Record of Corporate Judgements* is designed to support the final inspection team meeting by moving from the detail of what was known before the inspection, through the evidence base collected during the inspection, to the evaluation of the effectiveness of the school. In short, you are expected to use the *Record of Corporate Judgements* to bring all your judgements together and reach some overall conclusions.

The main strengths and weaknesses are expressed, in draft form, as they will appear in the relevant boxes in the summary of the inspection report, namely WHAT THE SCHOOL DOES WELL and WHAT COULD BE IMPROVED. The *Record of Corporate Judgements* also gives space to draft the matters that the 'appropriate authority' must include in its post-inspection action plan. These should match exactly the entries in the section WHAT COULD BE IMPROVED.

The final team meeting represents the culmination of the collection of evidence, testing out hypotheses and reaching tentative judgements, which are then confirmed, or otherwise. The *Record of Corporate Judgements* is a way of ensuring that the team's agreed judgements are recorded so that they can be used as the basis for writing the inspection report. Individual inspectors will be able to contribute a range of strengths or weaknesses in each section of the *Evaluation Schedule* and the team needs to weigh these up, making reference to the evidence base where necessary, to reach corporate judgements. Once these judgements have been agreed, it is a relatively easy task for the team to assign grades to the judgement recording statements.

You will also need to record the source from which the judgement stems. This might be a reference to an *Inspection Notebook* or it might be a reference to one or more *Evidence Forms*. If you refer to an *Inspection Notebook*, you will need to ensure that it contains the reference to the *Evidence Forms*.

You should use the *Record of Corporate Judgements* carefully and record only the significant points you wish to include in the inspection report. You should record all the required judgements you will need for the summary report, so that when you come to write it, all the necessary information will be to hand. When you, and in some cases others, come to write the commentary section of the report, you will need to expand these points, drawing on explanatory and illustrative material from *Inspection Notebooks* and *Evidence Forms*.

The school judgement recording form

You will need to end your discussions of each section of the *Evaluation Schedule* by grading the judgement recording statements relevant to your inspection. In SHORT INSPECTIONS, the statements will be those at the top of the list of statements, printed in bold typeface. In FULL INSPECTIONS, you will also need to grade the more detailed statements printed in italic typeface.

If assigning a grade is difficult, it probably indicates that a clear corporate judgement has not been reached and you are advised to go back to consider the judgement itself, making use of the strengths, weaknesses and illustrations contributed by members of the inspection team. Having reconsidered the judgement, and possibly having re-written it in the *Record of Corporate Judgements*, the grade should fall naturally into place.

The ten judgement recording statements in the *Record of Corporate Judgements* not connected directly with an *Evaluation Schedule* heading (*P1–P10*) are pointers to what the report contains, not judgements in themselves. For example, *Statement P1* is not about whether the attainment of boys and girls is different, but about whether the report contains such a judgement. You can, therefore, usually answer these straightforwardly with *Yes* or *No*.

You will also need to consider as a team whether the grades in the *PICSI report* which describe the school's performance in relation to similar schools will be included in the report as they are printed in the *PICSI report* or if they will be modified. If you feel there is substantial and compelling evidence to suggest that a grade different by one grade from that given in the *PICSI report* is more appropriate, then this should be entered and an explanation given. If you feel that, in an exceptional case, a change of two or more grades, or the omission of the grade, is necessary, you must additionally inform the Inspection Quality Division of OFSTED of this, giving the reasons for your decision, and submit the supporting evidence.

Guidance on reaching conclusions about whether the school requires special measures, has serious weaknesses, or is underachieving, is given in Annex 2.

The summary of the extent of inspection evidence at the end of the *Record of Corporate Judgements* is completed by collating the times and evidence bases from each *Inspection Notebook* used. In SHORT INSPECTIONS, you will need to ask the other members of the inspection team to inform you of their contribution as it will not always be recorded in an *Inspection Notebook*.

Style of writing

Because the *Record of Corporate Judgements* is a summary of the team's inspection judgements, it should be written very concisely. It should consist of:

- single-sentence statements, or the equivalent in note form;
- coded references to *Inspection Notebooks* and *Evidence Forms*, using the entries in the bottom centre box at the top of each relevant *Evidence Form*.

7 How well is the school led and managed?

How effectively do the leadership and management of the school contribute to pupils' achievements?

Main strengths and weaknesses, indicating groups of pupils and Key Stages where relevant, and sources of evidence, and an overall evaluation.

Sources of evidence:

Strengths:

- Very dynamic leadership by HT ensuring significant school improvement through impressive leaps in NC test and GCSE examination results through his commitment to high standards and individual success since his appointment three years ago — *EFs, CB2, TJ8, 10, KF11, PIC*

- Clear and systematic development planning, closely linked to the previous inspection report, annual department reviews and good links with governors' financial planning — *EFs, TJ1, 10, CB4, PIC*

- Effective monitoring and evaluation, based on a rolling programme stemming from the SDP and centred on middle management responsibilities for standards and the quality of teaching — *EFs, KF7, 8, TJ12, CB4, 5, PIC*

- Energetic overview of COGB through active involvement in all school events and regular school visiting, including to classrooms, resulting in good knowledge of staff and pupils — *KF3, TJ12*

- Innovative use of financial planning to make best use of new technology and non-teaching staff — *CB4, TJ5, 6, PIC*

Weaknesses:

- Some unevenness in the incidence and quality of classroom lesson observation, e.g., MFL, GG — *EFs, CB9, 10, TJ3*

- Insufficient support for EAL co-ordinator — *KF5, 6*

Overall evaluation:

Leadership and management of the school are both effective and innovative, reflecting the close commitment to their responsibilities of the HT and COGB. Development planning is systematic and is fully costed. Weaker aspects are some aspects of delegation and the monitoring of a few departments.

Increasingly, inspections will take place in schools that are involved in a network, project or scheme which receives specific funding to promote particular educational goals such as raising standards.

The inspection report must refer to such involvement in the INFORMATION ABOUT THE SCHOOL section. You should also report on any impact on quality and standards in the school, which accrues from involvement in the project.

In some inspections, much more detailed evaluation of the project and its impact will feature through section 9 of the *Evaluation Schedule*. In such cases, additional time will be added to the inspection contract, and OFSTED will provide supplementary guidance on the inspection of the issue concerned.

This annex sets out background information about three initiatives in which some secondary schools are involved.

1. EARLY EXCELLENCE CENTRES

Purpose

Early Excellence Centres (EECs) aim to be models for the development of integrated early years services. They aim to bring together high-quality early learning, childcare and family support services for those children and parents who need them. They should be catalysts for the development of good practice in the areas and regions they serve, and for spreading new ideas and providing innovative services.

Key features

Early Excellence Centres usually incorporate one or more nursery schools or classes; occasionally, the local secondary school is involved in the partnership. EECs will:

- be multidisciplinary, by drawing together education, care, adult education, private and voluntary providers and employers to collaborate in providing one-stop services;

- have a strong emphasis on staff training and development, and outreach support for parents and other providers;

- include support for parents who need help with parenting skills and literacy, for example enabling parents to attend classes in the same centre as their children;

- allow parents who work or are training for work to have access to integrated education and childcare for their children;

- ensure that parents of children with special educational needs can look forward to early assessment of their child's needs and a planned programme of linked provision, including support for the parents themselves, where appropriate.

Inspection focus

You should evaluate only the direct impact of the activities of the EEC on the educational aspects of the secondary school you are inspecting, as set out in the *Evaluation Schedule*. Features may include the enhanced involvement of parents, students or others in the education provided. You must not evaluate the work or impact of other professional services, such as medical, social or psychological services, in relation to the school.

2. EDUCATION ACTION ZONES

Purpose

Education Action Zones (EAZs) are a key part of government policy to raise standards in areas which face challenging circumstances in terms of underachievement or disadvantage. They receive extra funding from government, business and industry. A partnership forum, which sets out an action plan to raise standards, runs them. They are freed from some statutory requirements.

Key features

Education Action Zones:

- are established in less favoured parts of the country;
- invite an innovative contribution from business;
- have government funding of at least £250,000 per annum matched by business funding;
- address local problems;
- focus on teaching and learning;
- may suspend the National Curriculum;
- could change teachers' pay and conditions;
- may employ Advanced Skills Teachers;
- are organised in different ways.

Centrally, they exist to raise educational achievement in the areas they serve.

Inspection focus

Evaluate how particular EAZ initiatives contribute to the effectiveness of the leadership and management of the school. For example, there may be:

- mentors from business working with headteachers;
- business expertise to improve teachers' skills at middle-management level;
- business help in target-setting.

You must evaluate the contribution of an EAZ against your assessment of its prime purpose, the likelihood or actuality of the EAZ raising standards achieved.

3. EXCELLENCE IN CITIES

Purpose

Excellence in Cities provides a new framework for inner-city schools. The initiative aims to raise standards and aspirations in bigger cities. It is designed to ensure that every gifted pupil is stretched and that a full range of special needs is met. The aim of the programme is to extend diversity and excellence by tackling low expectations and any other barriers to learning.

Key features

The initiative includes:

- a radical approach to the needs of gifted and talented children;
- an encouragement to schools to use setting to meet individual aptitudes and abilities;
- developing new tests to stretch the most able;
- tackling disruption in schools through learning support units;
- providing the support of learning mentors to every pupil who needs one;
- establishing new university summer schools for 16–17-year-olds in the inner-city.

Inspection focus

Like EAZs, the purpose of the initiative is to raise standards. If you are inspecting a school which is part of the Excellence in Cities initiative, your evaluation should give a clear view of the initiative's effect on the standards achieved and on any other factors which have an impact on standards, such as teaching and leadership and management. You should be able to identify positive benefits from the initiative across all aspects of the school. In particular, this should be evident in the standards achieved by gifted and talented pupils.

INDEX

Printed in the United Kingdom for The Stationery Office J0091737 C150 12/99